PROFILES OF FAITHFULNESS

Legacy Servants of
The Southwestern Baptist Theological Seminary

Edited by Alex Sibley
Foreword by Gregory A. Wills

Profiles of Faithfulness: Legacy Servants of
The Southwestern Baptist Theological Seminary
Edited by Alex Sibley
Copyright © 2019 by Seminary Hill Press

Seminary Hill Press (SHP) is the publishing arm of The Southwestern Baptist
Theological Seminary, 2001 West Seminary Drive, Fort Worth, Texas 76115.

Layout/design by Caitlyn Jameson.

ISBN-13: 978-1-7327740-3-2

CONTENTS

Foreword   v

Introduction   1

1. B.H. Carroll   4

2. L.R. Scarborough   12

3. J.B. Gambrell   20

4. George W. Truett   26

5. J. Frank Norris   34

6. W.T. Conner   42

7. I.E. Reynolds   48

8. J.M. Price   54

9. T.B. Maston   60

10. Floy Barnard   66

11. E.D. Head   70

12. J. Howard Williams   76

13. Robert E. Naylor   82

14. John Earl Seelig   88

15. Roy J. Fish   92

16. William B. Tolar   98

Resources for Further Study   103

FOREWORD

This is a book of remembrance. It recalls lives spent in faithful service to establish and sustain The Southwestern Baptist Theological Seminary.

Remembering is fundamental to living a faithful life. Throughout the Scriptures, God commanded His people to remember and not to forget.

God grounded some of His commands in history. Five times in the book of Deuteronomy, God appeals to Israel's former status as slaves as a basis for their observance of the Sabbath, of the Feast of Weeks, and for their treatment of the poor, the alien, orphans, and widows— "Remember that you were a slave in Egypt, and the Lord your God redeemed you from there. Therefore I am commanding you to do this" (Deuteronomy 5:15; 15:15; 16:12; 24:18, 22).

God commanded His people to remember His judgments in order to strengthen them against disobedience and distrust—"Remember what the Lord your God did to Miriam on the journey after you left Egypt" (Deuteronomy 24:9). Jesus commanded His disciples to "Remember Lot's wife" (Luke 17:32).

God called His people to trust Him by calling them to remember His merciful deeds in the past—"Remember the wondrous works he has done, his wonders, and the judgments he has pronounced" (Psalm 105:5; 1 Chronicles 16:12).

God called His people to remember His judgments and work in order that they might stand immoveable, to worship and obey Him alone—"Remember this and be brave; take it to heart, you transgressors! Remember what happened long ago, for I am God, and there is no other; I am God, and no one is like me. I declare the end from the beginning, and from long ago what is not yet done" (Isaiah 46:8-10a).

What God has done in the past informs our duty in the present. When we remember, we are called to renounce pride and self-sufficiency. When we remember, we are warned and restrained from disobedience. When we remember, we are encouraged and strengthened to trust God's Word. When we remember, we are renewed in zeal for His service.

Those remembered in this volume are memorials to God's faithfulness to us and to former generations. They remind us that we are indebted to them. We benefit from their labors and sacrifices. We receive instruction and wisdom from them. We are encouraged and strengthened by their example.

Let us render our thanksgiving to God for them and for this seminary. Encouraged by their example, let us deepen our resolve to advance the purposes for which this seminary exists—to serve our Savior with faithful labor and unflagging zeal for the advance of the Gospel and the strengthening of His church.

It is good to remember.

Gregory A. Wills
Research Professor of Church History and Baptist Heritage
Director, B.H. Carroll Center for Baptist Heritage and Mission
The Southwestern Baptist Theological Seminary
Fort Worth, Texas

INTRODUCTION

The name "Southwestern Baptist Theological Seminary" evokes more than a physical campus in Fort Worth, Texas; more than an institution of higher education; and even more than a training ground for ministers of the Gospel. While the name certainly evokes each of those things, it also calls to mind the insurmountable legacy of thousands who have walked the grounds of this great school in the Southwest and given their lives for Kingdom service.

Adam W. Greenway, the ninth president of Southwestern Seminary, says that when students come to the historic Fort Worth campus to prepare for ministry, they enter into "a storyline of Gospel faithfulness that transcends generations." He refers not only to the numerous alumni who have come here and then gone forth better equipped for ministry in order to live their calling, but also to the men and women who have invested their lives in the seminary itself—those who founded it, and those who stewarded its vision in the decades that followed. He refers to the legacy of these great servants of Christ who gave years of their lives that others might have a more faithful ministry for Christ and the church.

This volume profiles just some of these individuals from the history of Southwestern Seminary—the men and women who made the institution what it is today. As Dr. Greenway has said since his presidency began, today's students and faculty are living in a house they did not build, drinking from a well they did not dig. This volume highlights some of the men and women who built the house and dug the well.

This project began as a series of articles published on the Southwestern Seminary website. Initially intended as a summer project, when we began delving into the history of these great men and women of God, we discovered an exceedingly rich heritage of Gospel faithfulness that pointed to a great and faithful God who formed and sustained the seminary over these 111 years. We therefore determined that compiling these profiles into a single volume would behoove readers interested in Southwestern Seminary's history, as well as those considering entering into this "storyline of Gospel faithfulness."

The individuals chosen are representative of countless more who could have been covered. We make no claim to have provided exhaustive coverage of all the men and women who made Southwestern Seminary into the "crown jewel" seminary of the Southern Baptist Convention. But these here are included because of their significant contributions to the development of the institution, and we pray you will be encouraged by how God used each of these individuals to make an impact not just on Southwestern Seminary, but for the Kingdom.

Special thanks for this volume are due to Hannah Roberts-Antunes for proposing the original idea for this project; to Jill Botticelli and Charles Huckaby of Southwestern Seminary's Archives for compiling the list of resources for further study at the end of this volume; to Robert A. Baker, whose 75-year history of Southwestern Seminary, *Tell the Generations Following*, proved an invaluable resource in our research; and to Adam Covington and Colby Adams for their editorial oversight.

Alex Sibley
Managing Editor, Seminary Hill Press
Associate Director of News and Information
The Southwestern Baptist Theological Seminary
Fort Worth, Texas

PROFILES of FAITHFULNESS

B.H. CARROLL

Traveling by rail through the Texas Panhandle, B.H. Carroll looked across the plains and saw a vision of the Baptist situation in the Southwest. He saw multitudes of preachers with limited education; consecrated men hungering for better training in the work to which God called them and to which they had dedicated their lives. He saw many institutions in the Southwest for the training of teachers, lawyers, doctors, and farmers, but not a single institution dedicated to the training of Baptist preachers. "It weighed upon my soul like the earth on the shoulders of Atlas," he later wrote.

Carroll seemed to hear God question, "Whom shall I send, and who will go for me?" Carroll was ready to give Isaiah's answer: "Here am I; send me."

"But at once there arose before me what seemed insuperable obstacles," Carroll writes.

He began to think of the many struggling institutions of other important and necessary lines of Baptist work, and "the heavy burdens that these institutions had placed upon the shoulders of our pioneer people." He thought, as well, of his advanced age and declining health, supposing that he could "hardly hope to live long enough to consummate such a gigantic enterprise," let alone serve as its leader. It occurred to him, also, that much of his life had been given to promoting denominational enterprises and that he had hoped to give his last years to "the quiet, unmolested companionship of my books."

Carroll was thus ready to dismiss the matter, feeling that he could not do it.

"[But] there came to me as clearly as if audibly spoken the assuring word of our Lord: 'I am He that liveth, and was dead, and behold, I am alive for evermore,'" Carroll writes. "With this trumpet-tongued call and assurance of divine help resounding in every part of my being, I wrestled with the problem until at last I was irresistibly driven to say, 'Lord, it is clearly thy will; what is impossible with man is possible with God; go thou with me and I will try.'"

When Carroll came to himself there on the train, he realized he had stood and tightly gripped the seat before him. Other passengers stared at him in amusement, unaware of the monumental occasion they had just witnessed. Carroll returned to his seat, embarrassed.

"But from that hour I knew as definitely as I ever knew anything, that God would plant a great school here in the Southwest for the training of our young Baptist preachers," he writes.

That school would be The Southwestern Baptist Theological Seminary, founded in 1908 and located since 1910 in Fort Worth, Texas. This train-ride vision, occurring in the spring of 1905, would lead to the equipping of more than 46,000 God-called men and women to touch the world and impact eternity over the course of the next century and beyond. And it was to the founding of this great institution that the 61-year-old Carroll would devote the rest of his life.

Benajah Harvey Carroll was born in 1843 in Carrollton, Mississippi. By his own admission, he remained a spiritual "infidel" for much of his early life, but finally came to know the Lord through a revival meeting at age 21. He quickly became a zealous and powerful preacher of the Word of God, and devoted his life to Christian service.

Carroll pastored multiple churches, spending 28 years as pastor of the First Baptist Church of Waco; he was instrumental in the formation of the Baptist General Convention of Texas (BGCT) and in the consolidation of the two Texas Baptist colleges into Baylor University; he was a leading voice when controversies arose within the Southern Baptist Convention; he served as a trustee of both Baylor University and Southern Baptist Theological Seminary in Kentucky; and he served as a professor and then dean of the Bible Department at Baylor. He was also involved in numerous fundraising endeavors for Baptist causes.

By 1905, after a life of service, Carroll was in declining health and nearly deaf. Perhaps understandably, he looked forward to retirement. But after receiving his train-ride vision from the Lord, he realized that his greatest work remained to be done: founding a school for the training of Gospel ministers in the Southwest.

"It started with no endowment and with no prospect of any," says L.R. Scarborough, Carroll's assistant and later successor as president of Southwestern Seminary. "No convention and no denominational board guaranteed its support; no wealthy patron financially guaranteed its life. It had no habitat.

"It had the guarantees only that were mixed in the faith and in the heart of one giant preacher, and in the hearts of his loyal supporters, whose number was not large at that time. His faith challenged the resources of God and lashed the program and future development of the seminary to God."

Despite the arduousness of the task, or perhaps because of it, Carroll wasted no time in seeking to fulfill his vision. Before returning from his journey, he had already begun efforts to raise $30,000, which he felt would provide for salaries and expenses of a seminary staff for three years. He made a list of 100 friends, then wrote each of them a personal letter asking for $100 a year as an emergency fund for the proposed seminary. By the end of that summer, he had pledges and cash in the amount of $22,000.

Carroll strategically worked with Baylor's board of trustees in order to launch the school, and it initially emerged in the fall of 1905 as Baylor Theological Seminary in Waco. Carroll and Baylor's leadership later agreed, however, that the seminary should exist as a distinct institution from the university. The school thus emerged as The Southwestern Baptist Theological Seminary on March 14, 1908, when it was formally chartered. Carroll was named the seminary's president.

In its first semester, Southwestern Seminary matriculated 190 ministerial students, together with laymen and women preparing for special Christian service, for a total enrollment of 215. They had come from four foreign countries and 11 states and territories.

As president, Carroll's primary responsibilities were helping to sustain the ministerial students in the school and soliciting funds to keep the school in operation. In addition to teaching at the school, lecturing across multiple states, and overseeing the faculty, Carroll thus devoted great efforts to writing individual appeals.

Even after suffering a severe fall in the summer of 1908 that left him confined to his room, Carroll did not remain idle, but constantly wrote letters seeking funds to finance the seminary.

In one such letter to a Texas pastor, Carroll wrote, "I am up a tree. Can you and your fine men help me?" The pastor replied, "I'm in a hole. How can a man in a hole help a man up a tree?" Carroll answered, "When you come up the tree to help me down, you will be out of your hole."

Beyond founding the institution itself, seeking to provide for its continuing operation, and assembling the faculty, one of Carroll's most significant contributions to Southwestern Seminary was his establishment of a chair of evangelism, which he called "the Chair of Fire."

"There is great need to create and endow a chair of evangelism," he said in a 1906 report to the Southern Baptist Convention. "Revivals are not only the hope of a lost world but the hope of the churches. If a seminary have not the mind of the Lord, it is none of His. If the Spirit of the Lord do not indwell it, it is a vacant house."

"The mind and spirit of Jesus appear in His life," he continued. "His school of the prophets was intensely practical. The wisdom He inculcated was the winning of souls."

The Chair of Fire at Southwestern Seminary, established in 1908, was the first chair of evangelism at any seminary in North America. Its first occupant and later namesake was L.R. Scarborough.

"Many times [Carroll] appealed to me to accept the position in the seminary in a way that swept my soul," Scarborough recalled. "What I owe to B.H. Carroll in compassion for lost men as he interpreted the embodiment and compassion of Christ for lost men I can never tell. He made Christ's love for men real to me and to all those to whom he preached."

By 1909, Carroll and Southwestern Seminary's board of trustees agreed that the institution should move to its own location (rather than remain part of Baylor University's campus in Waco). The infant seminary ultimately moved to Fort Worth, Texas, in 1910. But though the seminary now had its own home, its location was remote and not easily accessible, and its first building, Fort Worth Hall, would not be finished for several years.

Carroll was burdened by the plight of his students and faculty in having to operate in a still-under-construction building, but he commended them for bucking up under adverse circumstances. "Well, we plead no baby act and play no whining role," he wrote of the school's first semester in Fort Worth. "We have camped out before."

Throughout the seminary's early years, Carroll's health worsened. Beginning in the fall 1911 semester, Carroll could lecture only once a week. The remaining lectures he dictated to a stenographer in his bedroom; these were then reproduced by mimeograph and distributed to his students. His ongoing attempts to secure funds were similarly weakened.

At Carroll's request, Scarborough was appointed assistant to the president in 1913, essentially making him acting president and spokesman for the seminary. Carroll gradually became less involved with the day-to-day operations of the seminary and was mostly bedridden. In November 1914, roughly a month before his 71st birthday, Carroll fell into a coma for several days. He died on November 11.

"He was at the genesis of the institution," said Scarborough days after Carroll's death. "He saw it in vision. He planned it, nurtured it, formed its ideals, set its standards, projected its endowment, and contributed most largely to its spirit. It was born in his loving heart, and has grown up to its present strength feeding on his heart's blood. It is his dearest spiritual offspring. It is the crowning work of his last years."

Carroll had envisioned a great school in the Southwest for the training of young Baptist preachers. Within three years, that vision had become a reality. What was impossible with man was possible with God, and by faith, Carroll founded the seminary. He not only saw his vision fulfilled, but he led the seminary through its earliest days. More than 110 years later, more than 46,000 men and women have been trained for Gospel service because of how he spent his final years.

"We believe God has led us thus far that He may lead us on," Scarborough said. "We trust in God, and go forward to the task left us by our honored leader ... and will do our best to build it along the lines laid out by him, under the direction of the Spirit of God."

– Alex Sibley

L.R. SCARBOROUGH

B.H. Carroll was dying. Though his students and colleagues would later affectionately call him "the immortal B.H. Carroll" as a testament to his ongoing spiritual influence, as far as his earthly residence was concerned, his time was drawing to a close.

"My greatest concern is not for myself," Carroll said as he lay on his deathbed in one of his last conversations on earth. "My spiritual horizon is cloudless. The way up to the fellowship of Christ and the redeemed is clear. But my deep concern is about the seminary."

The visionary, founder, and first president of The Southwestern Baptist Theological Seminary, Carroll was leaving big shoes to fill, and he knew the appointment of a worthy successor was of utmost importance. Carroll had founded the seminary; now it needed a steward who could grow its student body, expand its physical campus, imbue it with fiery passion for the lost, and oversee the training of its students for Gospel-centered service. For this herculean task, Carroll personally picked as his successor L.R. Scarborough.

Looking at Scarborough's childhood—he grew up on a ranch in the western frontier of Texas and proved himself a talented cowboy—he may not have seemed the obvious choice for the position of seminary president. So what happened in Scarborough's intervening years to bring him from rustic cowboy to Carroll's first and only choice for stewarding his great vision of a "school of the prophets" in the Southwest?

The answer is that God used a myriad of individuals—including Carroll himself—to touch, influence, equip, and encourage Scarborough and lead him on a path from cowboy to student to preacher/evangelist to pastor to professor and, ultimately, to seminary president. Numerous individuals left their mark on Scarborough so that he could later leave his mark on Southwestern Seminary.

Lee Rutland Scarborough was born on July 4, 1870, and just three weeks later, his mother prayed over his cradle that God would someday call him to preach. In the years that followed, she and her husband, a Baptist preacher, made their home as conducive as possible to each of their children becoming followers of Christ.

Under his parents' spiritual influence, Scarborough professed faith in Jesus Christ as his Lord and Savior at the age of 17. Acknowledging his parents' role in this decision, Scarborough later said, "I count as the richest inheritance of my life that which my father and mother left me and the other children in faithful lives of consecration and service to God and humanity."

For the first 16 years of Scarborough's life, his family lived on a ranch. There, Scarborough worked as a cowboy and became adept at roping, horseback riding, and handling a six-shooter. This chapter of Scarborough's life ended, however, when his family moved to a new city in 1886 and he began attending school full-time.

Scarborough soon developed the desire to become a lawyer. At that point, his parents again proved greatly impactful. The elder Scarboroughs had saved money over the years to build themselves a proper home, but when their son became of age to go to college, they realized this money would be better spent in sending him to school instead. They did so, and Scarborough went to Baylor University in Waco to pursue his bachelor's degree.

Before he left, Scarborough's father made him promise to attend every Sunday the First Baptist Church of Waco—where B.H. Carroll was pastor—and write home an outline of Carroll's sermon along with everything else he could remember from the message. Scarborough honored this promise, and though his initial reports were brief, as he continued to sit under Carroll's powerful preaching, they soon became more extensive, sometimes spanning 40 or 50 pages.

"That was my course in systematic theology, Bible exposition, homiletics, evangelism, missions, and in denominational co-operancy—a whole seminary course from the pulpit of the First Baptist Church of Waco," Scarborough said.

Scarborough graduated from Baylor in 1892. He then enrolled in Yale to pursue a second bachelor's degree, still intending to become a lawyer—despite his mother's cradle-side prayer and his father's insistence that God had called him to preach. Scarborough initially resisted his parents' pleas, but while he attended Yale, God's calling eventually proved both undeniable and irresistible.

"I offered God every excuse I could," Scarborough said. "He would take none of them. 'Preach, preach!' He seemed to cry in my heart. ... The load was too heavy. I cried, 'I surrender: take me, Lord Jesus, and use me anywhere. Just give me the chance and I'll preach.'"

Scarborough returned home and immediately began preaching. He was eventually called to pastor the First Baptist Church of Cameron, Texas. He left for a time to attend Southern Baptist Theological Seminary in Louisville, Kentucky, but he later returned to Cameron. Then, from 1901-1908, Scarborough pastored the First Baptist Church of Abilene, Texas.

In both churches, Scarborough's ministry was characterized by evangelistic zeal and passion for the Word. Both churches saw growth in their congregations, and Scarborough, sometimes appealing to his cowboy days in order to relate to those in the community, baptized numerous individuals.

By 1905, B.H. Carroll had his vision for Southwestern Seminary, and he sought to establish within it a chair of evangelism, the first such academic chair in any seminary. As to the chair's first occupant—the man who would lead Southwestern Seminary's evangelism department both academically and by example, as well as produce evangelism literature that would kindle in the hearts of students, churches, and the entire denomination a passionate concern for New Testament soul-winning—Carroll had a specific person in mind: L.R. Scarborough.

Though Scarborough initially declined Carroll's invitation from a desire to remain in the pastorate, over time, he realized the opportunity was too great to ignore.

"Three things are as clear to me as the noon-day," Scarborough later said—"my acceptance of Christ and Christ's acceptance of me in my salvation; my call to the ministry; and God's placement of me in the seminary."

In 1908, Scarborough became the first occupant of Southwestern Seminary's Chair of Evangelism, nicknamed "the Chair of Fire." In this role, Scarborough taught courses on evangelism and produced such texts as *Recruits for World Conquests* and *With Christ After the Lost*—cornerstones of the seminary's evangelism curriculum for many years.

In addition to his teaching responsibilities, Scarborough also served as field secretary for the seminary, which primarily meant assisting Carroll in raising funds for the institution. Scarborough was also instrumental in relocating the seminary from its original home in Waco to Fort Worth in 1910, and then overseeing the construction of its first building, Fort Worth Hall.

During this period, Scarborough also initiated discussions with the Baptist Women Mission Workers of Texas regarding the construction of a building for a Women's Training School on the seminary campus (which would be fulfilled in the construction of Barnard Hall four years later).

By 1913, Carroll had become too ill to perform many of his duties, so trustees named Scarborough assistant to the president. This, in effect, made him acting president and spokesperson for the seminary until Carroll's death the following year.

As his time drew near, Carroll knew he wanted Scarborough to succeed him as Southwestern Seminary's president. From his deathbed, he shared with Scarborough, a protégé of his since Scarborough's time at Baylor, his heart for the seminary's future.

"My deep concern is about the seminary," Carroll told him. "Your life will be given largely to it. ... Keep the fires of love burning on all the altars about the seminary. Faith, prayer, and love will bring the money and keep the enduring elements around it. These will have to save it.

"Keep it on a hot trail after the lost. That is why I started the Chair of Evangelism and chose you as its professor. Never let it get away from the compassion of Calvary. Keep it missionary and true to the truth. Give it the best of your life."

Carroll died in November 1914, and Scarborough was inaugurated as Southwestern Seminary's second president the following February. As steward of Carroll's legacy for the next 27 years, Scarborough sustained the infant seminary during difficult times and championed its development into one of the greatest theological seminaries in the world.

During his tenure, Scarborough oversaw the construction of Barnard Hall and Cowden Hall; the formation of the schools of church music and religious education; and the transfer of the ownership of the seminary from the Baptist General Convention of Texas to the Southern Baptist Convention, thus strengthening ties between Southwestern Seminary and the denomination. Scarborough also led the seminary through the financial difficulties stemming from the Great Depression of the 1930s, employing such radical strategies to keep the seminary afloat as investing in South Texas citrus orchards.

Despite his heightened focus on administrative matters, Scarborough continued teaching throughout his presidency, investing in some 8,000 students during that time. He also maintained his focus on evangelism, declaring that "the entire administration and teaching force, the whole life of the institution, is set to the high notes of soul-winning." Scarborough led by example, remaining a personal soul-winner and preaching numerous revivals.

One contemporary of his recalled a time when Scarborough received a late-night phone call from a man who had heard Scarborough preach a revival several months earlier and desired then to be saved. Scarborough drove across snowy, icy roads to the man's home, arriving at 2:30 a.m. The man revealed that this was a test—if Scarborough came, then he truly cared about him and his words were real; but if Scarborough waited until the weather conditions softened, then the man would make no profession of faith. Having demonstrated the sincerity of his heart and genuineness of his message, Scarborough led the man to Christ.

Scarborough's contemporary remarked, "I imagine that on his return drive to Fort Worth, the weather was warm and the roads seemed clear—made so by the 'Chair of Fire.'"

Scarborough retired in 1942, having gone from West Texas cowboy to seminary president in the span of his lifetime. Regarding how such a transformation took place, Scarborough's foreword to *With Christ After the Lost* provides a window into his thoughts on the matter.

Referring to himself in the third-person, Scarborough writes, "The author herein acknowledges a debt of gratitude to the immortal B.H. Carroll, under the influence and inspiring example of whose evangelistic ministry he was placed for many years; to his devoted preacher father, under whose soulful sermons and inspiring life he learned to love lost men; to a sainted mother, whose prayers were answered in his call to preach and by whose efforts he was led to see himself a sinner and to find Christ as Savior...."

Scarborough proceeds to name various other individuals, including his wife Neppie, who impacted his life and ministry over the years, indicating the significance of fellow believers making their mark on his life. As a result of their investment, Scarborough was able to make his mark on Southwestern Seminary, with the Chair of Fire and the institution's college later bearing his name.

Now, 111 years after Scarborough joined the Southwestern Seminary faculty, more than 46,000 students have gone forth from the institution, and many more continue to do so, in order to make their mark on the world. These students have many people to thank for the existence of such an institution, but surely among the chief recipients of this gratitude is the immortal L.R. Scarborough.

– Alex Sibley

J.B. GAMBRELL

In 1841, a boy like any other was born in Anderson, South Carolina. He grew of age on a farm in Mississippi and attended country schools. By any standard, they were unremarkable boyhood years. But make no mistake—James Bruton Gambrell was born to be a fighter.

J.B. Gambrell accepted the call of Christ at a revival meeting in 1856, at age 15. He had a noteworthy thirst for books, and he familiarized himself with all the books available within several miles of his home. His parents envisioned a good education for their son, but the Civil War interrupted, and at 20, he volunteered in the Confederate Army, serving for 28 months as a scout for Robert E. Lee, distinguishing himself by his daring exploits.

On one of his expeditions, he met Mary Corbell in Nansemond County, Virginia. A year later, he returned and slipped through enemy lines, and they were married at midnight. The war shaped many men, but few were more dynamic than the scout who snuck behind enemy lines to steal away his beautiful bride. In 1867, after the close of the war, Gambrell began preaching, returning to his unremarkable beginnings— the church where he spent his boyhood.

But war had stirred a fervent can-do spirit that would shape his life's work. Gambrell would go on to define institutions that served Baptists at the local and national levels, fighting for Baptist ideals. He fought for The Southwestern Baptist Theological Seminary, for the Baptist General Convention of Texas, for world initiatives, and, above all, for the souls of men.

"You are fighting the devil for a soul, and you can't afford to be impatient," he wrote in his essay "Up Fool Hill." Persistent, and straightforward, he ever was.

In 1870, Gambrell began the practice of writing every day. When The Baptist Record, the newspaper of the Mississippi Baptist Convention, was launched, Gambrell was named its editor, aiding in the development of a strong denominational consciousness. While affirming local autonomy, Gambrell urged Southern Baptists to unite toward global evangelism. In 1881, he moved the paper to Clinton, Mississippi, where a church selected him as pastor.

There, Gambrell threw himself into the fight to drive away saloons. In 1887, his son, Roderick Dhu Gambrell, a journalist who also crusaded against the liquor trade, was assassinated in the streets of Jackson, Mississippi. The leader of the liquor forces was found not guilty, and a mob collected to punish the acquitted man. Gambrell made a powerful plea to the mob to disperse, fighting to save the life of the man who had killed his own son.

Gambrell toiled on. In 1890, J.M. Frost of Virginia began advocating for the organization of a Sunday School board for the Southern Baptist Convention (SBC). Though Gambrell opposed it, they wrote a joint report that was unanimously adopted, and in May 1891, Frost founded the Baptist Sunday School Board, which later became LifeWay Christian Resources. "Baptists talk themselves together," Gambrell said.

In 1893, Mercer University in Macon, Georgia, elected Gambrell its president. Three years later, the Baptist General Convention of Texas (BGCT) was being torn apart by critics and had no official leader; Gambrell felt the call to go. Directors held an all-night prayer meeting and chose as secretary a little-known man from Georgia: at age 55, Gambrell was elected unanimously, and he served 13 years. Gambrell made an immediate impact on Texas Baptist life and was heralded as a brilliant organizer and motivator.

In 1907, the BGCT unanimously approved the founding of The Southwestern Baptist Theological Seminary, and Gambrell—along with D.I. Smyth and A.J. Barton—applied for its charter. Gambrell was elected president of its board of trustees, stepping up to lead during the seminary's fledgling years, a role he filled from 1908-1912.

Beyond such formative tasks as overseeing the election of Southwestern Seminary's first president and faculty, Gambrell steered the immense task of picking up the young school from its home in Waco and transporting it to Fort Worth in 1910. Furthermore, he twice enriched the seminary faculty as a professor of ecclesiology—first from 1912-1914, then from 1916-1921. He remained connected with Southwestern Seminary for the rest of his life, inspiring a zeal for evangelism among its student body.

Gambrell pressed a vigorous schedule, teaching four days a week, then spending two days in the offices of The Baptist Standard, the BGCT's newspaper, where he had been named editor. He had a firm view of liberty of speech and argued vigorously that no one should be denied the right to preach his doctrine. "We would be willing to fight so that Catholics, Presbyterians, infidels, and all sorts might have freedom of thought and freedom of speech," he wrote in 1909.

In 1910, Gambrell retired from the BGCT; four years later, he was called back and served two more years. Its education board had been merged with its board of directors, and the combined administrative work was heavy for a man of 73. After that term, he declined re-election.

In 1917, Gambrell began three terms as SBC president, laboring during a period of economic and social reconstruction in the South. In 1920, a precedent of many years was broken, and Gambrell was elected for the fourth time as president.

Gambrell was a strong supporter of the foreign missionary enterprise, and in July 1920, he attended the London Conference of Baptists, representing the SBC. The meeting launched a fund to support missionary work in Europe. Gambrell regarded this conference as the most far-reaching in significance of any meeting the Baptists ever held. After its close, he and educator E.Y. Mullins visited Baptists throughout England and Europe. Gambrell exerted himself tirelessly; he did not know that his heart was weak.

In December, they returned home. Gambrell accepted many invitations, going at full stride. On February 24, 1921, he arrived by train in Fort Worth and decided to walk uptown. On the way, he suffered a heart attack from which he would never fully recover.

Gambrell returned to Dallas and was bedridden—except on Sunday, May 29, 1921, when he attended a service at First Baptist Church to hear J.H. Rushbrooke, Baptist World Alliance commissioner, preach. It was his last public appearance. He weakened until June 10, 1921, when he died at home.

Today, with his name attached to numerous public sites, including a street on the Southwestern Seminary campus, Gambrell's fighting spirit has been immortalized, and his words remain an encouragement to all Southern Baptists: "God's Word is plain. A Baptist has only to read and obey. He need not be a scholar, or a philosopher, though he may be both. He has no trouble to explain away what is written. He can read it and go by it without embarrassment.

"He can afford to be plain, simple, straightforward, and obedient. … I am a Baptist because John was, Jesus was, the apostles were, the first churches were, and all the world ought to be."

- Julie Owens

GEORGE W. TRUETT

During the early 20th century, George W. Truett would become one of the most renowned preachers, sought out for his teaching and spiritual leadership. He was a commanding and influential figure, yet he often described his role as the "humblest little spot in all the world." Though he would become known for his oratory skills, as a young teacher and principal for a remote Georgia mountain school, Truett's sights were set elsewhere, and he never thought much of his speaking abilities.

Yet it was during a gathering of the 1888 Georgia Baptist State Convention that a young and unassuming Truett was called to give an impromptu speech before a group of leaders and plead the case for financial support of rural mountain schools and their students seeking further education.

"Brethren, this is George Truett. He can speak like Spurgeon," said the Reverend Fernando C. McConnell. "George, tell them what the Lord has done for you, and what you are trying to do up in the mountains."

In the two years prior, the 18-year-old Truett had begun teaching in a one-room school and then founded the Hiawassee Academy, a rural mountain school where he served as principal. Truett viewed teaching as a special opportunity to pass on his love for knowledge to other students while simultaneously earning money to fund a future law degree.

Initially embarrassed by the invitation to stand before the Georgia leaders, once Truett began to speak, he quickly found his voice, advocating for the aspiring young people of the mountains.

As Truett shared his own experiences learning and teaching in that very region, the audience quickly realized the natural talent of the speaker before them. Truett's voice was steady and commanding as he delivered a message so compelling that men immediately opened their pocketbooks to ensure the future of mountain schools.

This same man who could "speak like Spurgeon" and who had moved an entire room of men to action would later go on to command the attention of millions worldwide. Truett's seemingly natural and God-given ability to inspire men and women to act would be a hallmark of his 50-year ministry as preacher and denominational leader. Truett had a global reach and was influential in the Southern Baptist Convention, but he always had a special relationship with Texas Baptists, including The Southwestern Baptist Theological Seminary.

In his earlier years, Truett continued to receive praise for his keen ability to capture the attention of a crowd like any of the best preachers. But Truett was never one to accept such praise, a characteristic he learned from his childhood years in South Carolina.

Among the many Christian influences in his life, Truett's mother was likely the greatest. Truett often found his mother praying for the salvation of her children and husband, and she later confessed that she often prayed for God to call Truett to the ministry. In answer to those fervent prayers, Truett professed faith in Christ at age 18 and would eventually forgo a career in law to pursue ministry.

Truett eventually followed his family to Texas, where he joined the Whitewright Baptist Church in Whitewright, Texas. Truett taught Sunday School and regularly filled in on Sundays when the pastor was away, and it was not long before these Texas congregants noticed the same gift first witnessed by those Georgia pastors.

Church members often discussed his talent amongst themselves and even told Truett he ought to be a preacher. Even so, Truett maintained that he aspired to be a lawyer.

However, the congregation was convinced that it was God's will for Truett to be a preacher. During a Saturday church meeting in 1890, Truett entered the church sanctuary and immediately noticed the strange sight of a full room that was usually sparse for such meetings.

During the meeting, a deacon made a motion that "this church call a presbytery to ordain Brother George W. Truett to the full work of the

Gospel ministry." The motion was promptly seconded, and the people voted in favor of Truett's ordination.

Shocked and embarrassed by this act, Truett stood before the church and pled for them to wait six months to consider their course of action. But the church refused, replying that they could not wait another six hours.

"There I was, against the whole church, against a church profoundly moved," Truett said. "There was not a dry eye in the house—one of the supremely solemn hours in a church's life. I was thrown into the stream and just had to swim."

Around this time, Baylor University was searching for a financial agent to help correct a significant debt. Although Truett was inexperienced, his pastor, R.F. Jenkins, believed Truett could be the man for the task and could inspire Texas Baptists to offer their finances to the effort.

In a letter to B.H. Carroll (then a Baylor trustee and preacher in Waco, and eventual founder of Southwestern Seminary), Jenkins wrote, "There is one thing I do know about George W. Truett—wherever he speaks, the people do what he asks them to do."

Despite Carroll's eventual recommendation, the Baylor trustees saw Truett's youth and were prepared to immediately dismiss him. But before they could adjourn their meeting, Truett stood up and demanded that they at least let him make his case.

The trustees were so compelled by his speech that they reconsidered their decision and gave him the job. Jenkins was right—whenever Truett spoke, people did what he asked them to do.

Truett's new role at Baylor sparked a lifelong friendship between him and B.H. Carroll, and Truett even lived with the Carrolls before marrying Josephine Jenkins in 1894. Truett became a popular figure for Baylor professors and students, who would seek out his preaching whether at Truett's church or whenever he filled in for Carroll at the First Baptist Church of Waco.

As word spread about this skilled preacher, churches started calling Truett to be their pastor. He always refused their offers until the fall of 1897 when Truett began his 41-year pastoral ministry at the First

Baptist Church of Dallas, Texas. Under his leadership, new professions of faith were made nearly every Sunday, and the church grew from 715 members to more than 7,000.

As early as 1900, Truett had become a distinguished pastor even outside Texas and the Baptist denomination. He became so popular, in fact, that people would schedule him at least two years in advance to preach church services, revivals, convention sermons, and seminary addresses. He famously delivered his "Baptists and Religious Liberty" sermon from the steps of the U.S. Capitol in Washington, D.C., on May 16, 1920. More than 15,000 people gathered to hear the popular Dallas pastor, including the nation's political leaders and Southern Baptists gathered for their annual meeting.

Although he often preached to the masses, Truett was always willing to do what it took to reach even just the individual. During the entirety of his ministry, he devoted on average two mornings a week to writing letters to those who were not saved, presenting the Gospel to win them to Christ.

"I could not quit this holy task if I wanted to, and when I know how many I have been able to lead to Christ by it and see the constant appeals pouring in upon me, I could not quit if I could," Truett said.

These principles never changed, but the context of his ministry did change on occasion. During Truett's rise to national recognition, President Woodrow Wilson selected Truett and 19 other American preachers to go overseas for six months to "deliver their messages of patriotism and religion to the Allied armies" fighting in World War I.

The days were long as he delivered as many as six sermons a day, once writing to his wife about preaching to a crowd of 15,000 soldiers. "I would have gladly crossed the ocean and braved all the perils and hardships for what I have seen and felt today," Truett wrote. "Vast multitudes came to the side of our great Savior and King. Impossible to tell you how great it was. Never, never, can I get away from the greatness and blessedness of this day. To God be all the praise, forever!"

Throughout his ministry, Truett was content with his role as a pastor and had mostly avoided any official denominational positions. Truett preached the 1899 Southern Baptist Convention sermon and served on various committees, but he usually recommended others for official positions and responsibilities. However, during the 1927 SBC meeting in Louisville, Kentucky, Truett was elected president of the convention. He was then re-elected in 1928 and 1929.

Many were surprised by Truett's nomination and ultimate election due to his lack of administrative and parliamentary experience. Truett himself was surprised, stating after his election, "I appreciate the honor, but from my deepest heart, I had hoped it would never come to me."

Despite his inexperience, Truett proved to be a capable and successful leader. He was later selected to lead other entities, including the Baptist World Alliance.

Even after many years of accomplishments and accolades from an admiring world, Truett remained humble in his work and was especially devoted to serving Texas Baptists. He had befriended many Baptist leaders, including B.H. Carroll, who in 1905 had envisioned a new Baptist seminary in the American Southwest.

Truett became one of the founding trustees of this new seminary. In November of 1907, after the founding of a new school was approved by the Baptist General Convention of Texas, the trustees met in Truett's Dallas office to elect Carroll as president of the seminary, nominate and elect the faculty, and give the seminary its name—The Southwestern Baptist Theological Seminary.

Truett later chaired the committee to find a location for the seminary, which ultimately found a home in Fort Worth, Texas, in 1910. He remained on the board of trustees from the school's founding until his death in 1944, and he served as president of the board from 1931-1944.

Beyond his official duties as a trustee, Truett sought to guide ministers in their calling. He was a frequent chapel preacher, and he maintained friendships with seminary faculty and students.

In a sermon series to Southwestern Seminary students regarding the calling to preach, Truett warned against two great temptations: "the love of gain" and "the love of power." In his message, he said of this calling, "It is the most robust, it is the most vital, it is the most heroic, and it calls for character to match the cause that we espouse."

Though most of his days were devoted to his preaching ministry at First Baptist Dallas, Truett always maintained his desire to influence and help future ministers, even donating the majority of his 6,000-volume library to Southwestern Seminary after his death. To honor his years of service, Southwestern Seminary later named Truett Auditorium for him, and his portrait still hangs outside it to greet those who enter from the rotunda of the B.H. Carroll Memorial Building.

Even at the time of his death in 1944, Truett was still inspiring future ministers who looked to him as an exemplary preacher whose dynamic preaching they could model. They were inspired by his humility, they were inspired by his devotion to reach the lost, and they were inspired to "speak like Truett."

- Katie Coleman

J. FRANK NORRIS

History has forgotten the primary and pivotal role John Franklyn Norris (1877-1952) played in the establishing of The Southwestern Baptist Theological Seminary in its home on a hill in south Fort Worth in 1910. Norris, pastor of the First Baptist Church of Fort Worth (1909-1952), was a legendary leader in his day, and his church became the largest church in America. At the dedication of First Baptist's new auditorium 10 years into his pastorate in 1919, The Fort Worth Record reported, "Total attendance for the day was more than 12,000, with at least 2,000 turned away, and 200 converts were added to the church."

Norris' legacy is a strange mixture of both fact and fiction. His perplexing personality seemed to live a life of perpetual paradox. If ever a man lived up to his nickname, "The Texas Tornado," it was Norris.

He was one of the most colorful and controversial figures in Texas history. From both his pen and his pulpit, he would often swoop down out of a dark cloud, strike with dastardly force, and leave in his wake the ruins of lives and even legacies.

While most 20th-century Baptist historians have revered the likes of L.R. Scarborough and George W. Truett, they have likewise reviled the legacy of J. Frank Norris. But there is "the rest of the story" that begs to be recorded for posterity.

In the beginning, Norris was the consummate denominational loyalist. Tutored by the legendary B.H. Carroll at Baylor University, he was an honors graduate at the university and valedictorian of the Southern Baptist Theological Seminary's class of 1905. Upon graduation from seminary, he moved to Dallas, where he eventually became owner/publisher/editor of The Baptist Standard while still in his 20s.

This position afforded young Norris a visible platform to promote the work of Baptists throughout the state of Texas and catapulted him into denominational prominence.

Meanwhile, down in Waco at Baylor, Carroll had dreams of expanding the university's Bible department into a full-fledged seminary and moving it to the rapidly growing Dallas-Fort Worth area. Although Truett would later serve for years as a Southwestern Seminary trustee and board chair and would be memorialized by having the campus auditorium named in his honor, he originally tried to form a coalition, consisting of A.J. Barton, J.B. Gambrell, and S.P. Brooks, among others, to oppose and prevent Carroll's dream from coming to fruition.

According to historian H. Leon McBeth, Carroll "encountered massive opposition" from this Truett-led coalition of respected Texas Baptists. Even though he opposed the move, by the sheer power of his personality, Truett had been appointed chair of the committee to find a new site for the fledging institution. In hopes of dampening the spirit of the move, he recommended two small lots in the Oak Cliff section of Dallas, which infuriated Carroll.

In a letter dated March 30, 1909, Carroll let Truett know in no uncertain terms that he considered this recommendation an insult, and he did not intend the new seminary to be "A TWO BY FOUR INSTITUTION."

Norris seized the moment. He loved Carroll and had revered him since his days at Baylor. Norris began a series of weekly articles on the front page of The Baptist Standard promoting Carroll and the move of the seminary to a site made available by the city fathers of Fort Worth on a hill south of town.

Those opposing the seminary move became irate with Norris for his advocacy and what they considered to be an unbalanced approach in the weekly tabloid. Truett convened a gathering of the directors of the Standard to remove Norris as editor. Norris was not only editor, however, but the majority stockholder, so he, at the same time, convened a meeting of the stockholders and subsequently dismissed all the directors. Many point to this incident as the beginning of an open hostility between Truett and Norris that would ensue for decades.

Norris' campaign caught on and won the hearts and minds of Texas Baptists. Thus, at the annual state convention meeting at Truett's own First Baptist Church of Dallas in 1909, it was young Norris—not Truett—standing beside the tall and stately Carroll on the platform making the appeal for the move of the seminary to Fort Worth. As historian Robert A. Baker would later recount, Norris invoked in unbroken eloquence, "Not since Peter preached at Pentecost and baptized 3,000 converts has there been anything more glorious than the founding, endowing, and locating of Southwestern Baptist Theological Seminary."

Thus, what was destined one day to become the largest seminary in all the world found its new home on a hill in Fort Worth, and in no small part because of the efforts and influence of a young J. Frank Norris.

A few months later, upon the recommendation of Carroll, Norris was called to be the pastor of the First Baptist Church of Fort Worth. Once there in his new church, Norris set out to raise the money to undergird the seminary and to build its first building.

The Fort Worth Star-Telegram reported that Norris was in Fort Worth "to meet members of the church and to confer with the committee which is soliciting subscriptions for the Baptist Theological Seminary." Two days later, the same paper reported, "At the First Baptist Church, Dr. J. Frank Norris ... preached a strong sermon, presenting to his congregation the great benefit that the proposed big seminary would confer, not only on the church, but on the city and humanity and Christianity in general. He presented a strong case for the seminary and its location here, and his words fell on willing ears."

Norris helped raise the $100,000 needed to bring the seminary from Waco to Fort Worth. And, in fact, "Norris pledged to raise half that amount from the church, and he did."

He did not stop there. He was the driving force behind raising the $200,000 needed to build the fledging seminary's first building, named Fort Worth Hall in honor of its new hometown, and led the congregants of First Baptist Church to give half of that amount as well.

Norris served faithfully and loyally as a founding trustee of

Southwestern Seminary until after the death of Carroll. Ironically, after Carroll's death, the seminary and her new leader, L.R. Scarborough, would find themselves in the middle of the bull's-eye of some of Norris' most vocal and vitriolic attacks, beginning with the encroachment of the theory of evolution within Christian institutions of higher learning in the 1920s.

In early 1921, J.A. Rice, a professor at Southern Methodist University, began promoting a pro-Darwinian approach to creation. This led Norris on a war path. He was joined by Scarborough, and, together, their challenges and campaign led to Rice's resignation.

Soon thereafter, Baylor professor Grove Samuel Dow published a book entitled *Introduction to Sociology*. Within its pages, he blatantly argued in favor of the naturalistic evolutionary process. Norris launched an assault on this heretical teaching at the bastion of Baptist education, resulting in the firing of Dow and eight other professors. Norris wrongly assumed that Scarborough would join him in this fight, as he did with the one at SMU over the same issue. To his utter amazement, Scarborough and Truett remained silent and responded, "We don't want to have any stir up about this. ... You will ruin the 75 Million Campaign."[1] This perceived hypocrisy in valuing denominational loyalty over doctrinal fidelity added to the growing divide between Norris and the leaders of the Southern Baptist Convention in Norris' mind.

Some observers think that a deeper part of Norris' growing conflict with Scarborough and Southwestern Seminary was that Norris had hoped, even expected, to be the handpicked successor to his mentor, Carroll. He saw himself as the true recipient of the charge Carroll gave to Scarborough to "keep the seminary lashed to the cross." He sharply disapproved of many of the changes Scarborough made after the death of Carroll, particularly in moving away from the English Bible course that Carroll had implemented and to which he was intensely committed. Interestingly, when Norris later founded his own seminary, the Bible Baptist Seminary, he reduplicated almost exactly the English Bible

---

[1] The 75 Million Campaign was a national effort by Southern Baptists to raise $75 million over a five-year period for missions and ministry. Both Truett and Scarborough were national campaign leaders.

course of B.H. Carroll.

As the later decades of his life unfolded, Norris' mean-spirited nature began to increasingly reveal itself. He would often send telegrams to Truett in the midnight- and early-morning hours on Sunday to awaken him from his sleep before he was to preach the morning message. He resorted to sending the professors at Southwestern Seminary beautifully wrapped Christmas presents that were placed on their front porches, only for them to find that the boxes were filled with all types of rotten fruits.

As one conflict and controversy led to another, Norris drew his own circle smaller and smaller until he had shut out much of what could have been his wider influence and lasting legacy. In the end, however, he sought to make amends to those with whom he did battle. The Scarborough Archives at Southwestern Seminary contain loving letters Norris sent Scarborough as the former seminary president lay dying in his daughter's home in West Texas.

Raymond Barber, a student at Norris' seminary during the late 1940s and early 1950s, tells the story of taking Norris on a trip one particular morning. As it was, Barber had one of the only automobiles among the seminary students in those days. On a given morning and at an appointed time, Norris asked the young seminarian to pick him up at his office and take him on a brief journey. Barber, accompanied by his brother, Bob, picked up the pastor, and they noted as he stepped into the back seat that he had a beautiful bouquet of flowers in his hand. Rather abruptly, he then said, "Drive me out west of town."

They drove west of the city until they came to a cemetery. Norris instructed the boys to stay in the car. He walked out across the endless tombstones until he went over a small hill and could not be seen. After a half-hour, he returned to the car, instructing Barber to take him back to his office and for the two of them to hurry back to seminary classes. Barber revealed that upon dropping the pastor at the church office, they headed straight back to the cemetery. They journeyed across the hundreds of tombstones until they spotted the bouquet of flowers Norris had brought. They found them on the grave of Lee Rutland Scarborough.

Southwestern Seminary grew from its birth to become the largest seminary in the world, sending multiplied thousands of her graduates to the international mission fields, as well as pulpits of churches and teaching lecterns in colleges and seminaries too numerous to mention. Among J. Frank Norris' many accomplishments, none have had more lasting Kingdom value and impact than his tireless, bold, and strategic efforts in the establishing of The Southwestern Baptist Theological Seminary in Fort Worth, Texas.

- O.S. Hawkins

W.T. CONNER

W.T. Conner, a founding professor of The Southwestern Baptist Theological Seminary, is still recognized as one of Baptist history's truly great theologians. His enduring legacy to Southern Baptist life lies in his 39-year teaching career at Southwestern Seminary, always regarding theology with a down-to-earth view and a straightforward path to acceptance of Christ.

"In the classroom, he endeavored to make theology practical rather than speculative," historian Stephen M. Stookey writes in Conner's profile for the Texas State Historical Association. "In the faculty, his recommendations for prospective teachers were tantamount to administrative approval."

Conner distinguished himself as the preeminent Southern Baptist theologian during the 1930s and 1940s. "He was at home among both laymen and scholars," Stookey writes. "His lectures and books were written with the layman in mind, but they display an underlying academic depth and extensive knowledge of his field."

Conner's practical view of theology shaped literally thousands of preachers, missionaries, and teachers around the world, who still recalled his influence years after his death.

Walter Thomas Conner was born at Center (now Rowell), Arkansas, in 1877, the son of Philip Orlander and Frances Jane Monk Conner. The family moved to the West Texas community of Tebo (now Tye) eight miles west of Abilene when he was 15.

Because of restricted finances, Conner's attendance at the academy of Simmons College (now Hardin-Simmons University) and Baylor University was intermittent. He received an A.B. degree from Baylor in

1906. In 1907, he married Blanche Horne, a Baylor University classmate. Then, in 1908, he received both a Th.B. from Baylor Theological Seminary (which chartered in March 1908 as The Southwestern Baptist Theological Seminary) and an A.M. degree from Baylor University.

In order to prepare for a teaching post at Southwestern Seminary, Conner enrolled at Rochester Theological Seminary in 1908, then received a B.D. degree there in 1910. That year, he began teaching systematic theology at Southwestern Seminary, when the school moved from Waco to Fort Worth.

Conner later studied at the University of Chicago and Southern Baptist Theological Seminary in Louisville, Kentucky, where he received his Th.D. degree in 1916, writing his thesis on "Pragmatism and Theology"—turning his focus to practical theology and logic. Baylor University awarded Conner an honorary D.D. degree in 1920. Then, when Southern Seminary began to award the Ph.D. degree instead of the Th.D., Conner availed himself of the opportunity to upgrade his Th.D. to Ph.D. status with an additional thesis on the topic "The Idea of Incarnation in the Gospel of John" in 1931.

Conner was the first pastor of Seminary Hill Baptist Church (now Gambrell Street Baptist Church) in Fort Worth, and pastored Baptist churches at Eagle Lake, Rock Island, East Bernard, Blum, Rio Vista, Godley, and Handley. While a student at Rochester, he served as pastor of the Baptist church in Wheatville, New York.

"His theology reflects the influence of three former professors: Benajah H. Carroll of Baylor, A.H. Strong of Rochester, and E.Y. Mullins of Louisville," Stookey writes. But Conner's theology displayed his own acumen. "His theological works reflect a biblical rather than systematic approach."

Applying his practical view to theology, Conner believed that there are three conditions without which there can be no union of God's people in the world: spiritual unity, or the brotherhood of Christian believers ("Men can never get together in spiritual unity until they get together in Christ," he wrote in 1923); doctrinal unity ("on the great fundamental doctrines of Christianity there must be agreement"); and the organization of the church and the ordinances of baptism and the Lord's Supper.

"Every time a penitent sinner goes down into the water to be baptized, he is preaching the Gospel of salvation through a crucified and risen Redeemer," Conner wrote. "He thereby confesses himself a sinner and Christ as his Savior. Therefore, the form of baptism is important."

"Somebody says it is only a form, so why stickle for a form?" he continued. "It is a form, but we must remember that it is a form with a meaning, and the meaning lies in the form. Therefore, if the form be changed, the meaning is destroyed. There is no Christian baptism then apart from immersion, which pictures a burial and a resurrection."

In Conner's final years of teaching, he developed an increasing interest in the spiritual side of the Christian faith. "Some of us can recall in those last months that he expressed repeatedly some remarkable insights of an intense devotion personally to Jesus as Lord and Savior," writes Darold Morgan, a former student of Conner's who later served as executive director of the Southern Baptist Annuity Board.

"For these months, we studied some of the masterpieces of Christian devotional material," Morgan writes. "What a joy even today to recall listening both to the other students in the seminar and to Dr. Conner as he made such insightful comments on the material."

Conner's last year of teaching was 1949, when a debilitating stroke ended his extraordinary ministry of lecturing, writing, and preaching. "I had the unique privilege of being in his last group of doctoral students, and can recall to this day the shock that followed the announcement of his stroke, which ended his active involvement at Southwestern," Morgan says.

Conner lived for three years after his stroke, limited to a wheelchair and his bed. Morgan recalls that a report circulated around the campus that Conner had repeatedly asked his wife, "Why did God leave me like this?" One day, she responded, "Perhaps He left you this way so you could catch up on your praying."

"Later, as she checked on him in the late-night hours, she could tell he was awake, despite his eyes being closed," Morgan recalls. "His lips were moving in prayer, and she saw tears on his face as he was in prayer and worship, as always taking a straightforward path to commune with Christ."

"Over these 50-plus years in my own pilgrimage since those distant days at Southwestern," Morgan says, "I have heard preachers and teachers and others in numberless settings of seminaries, conventions, and worship services. But I have never been as moved as I was so many times in Dr. Conner's classes. Although his lectures and prayers were usually monotone, when he shifted gears into the excitement of a particular truth, he was for me beyond Moses and Elijah."

Conner died in 1952 and is buried in Fort Worth. Morgan recalls of his former professor: "There were moments when his eloquence was so overpowering, his logic so forceful, his devotion to Christ so apparent that the force of those moments are still alive and dynamic in me."

- Julie Owens

I.E. REYNOLDS

In 1915, L.R. Scarborough was elected The Southwestern Baptist Theological Seminary's second president, tasked with leading it to greatness in all areas of curriculum. At the annual meeting of the Southern Baptist Convention in Houston that spring, Scarborough met a gifted singer, I.E. Reynolds. Scarborough invited Reynolds to visit the Southwestern Seminary campus in Fort Worth and to sing two solos in a chapel service.

Reynolds' performances were stirring and impressive, and trustees elected him as Southwestern Seminary's music director. That fall, they reported to the SBC: "It has been felt by your board for some time that there was needed in the South a strong department in the theological education of Gospel music, so we have elected and put to work Professor I.E. Reynolds, a thoroughly equipped Gospel singer."

It was the first school of church music established by Baptists. Throughout his 30-year tenure, "Ike" Reynolds shaped the school toward its current level of excellence—proving through hard work and devotion to be the right man for a unique, trail-blazing job.

A church musician, teacher, composer, and conductor, Isham Emmanuel Reynolds was born to Winfield and Mary Reynolds in Shades Valley, Alabama, on September 27, 1879. He became a Christian at the age of 15 during a revival meeting, and as a youth, he trained diligently for his future calling. He taught himself to play the mandolin and attended singing schools; from his father, he learned the "fa sol la" syllables of the Sacred Harp singing style.

While working in a factory making brushes for cotton gins, Reynolds enrolled in music studies at Mississippi College in Clinton for a year. He began directing music at revival meetings, then enrolled as a student at Moody Bible Institute in Chicago, and then at Chicago Musical College. During this time, he also studied under private tutors in voice, theory, and composition. Reynolds followed this with correspondence courses from Siegel-Myers School of Music in Chicago to earn a Bachelor of Music.

In 1910, the SBC's Home Mission Board began to employ evangelists and singers to conduct revivals throughout the South. Reynolds was among the first group of 43 musicians who served under that program through 1928.

These experiences were hardly conventional preparation for the director of a seminary music school. But all roads led to his appointment at Southwestern Seminary in 1915. The seminary's music program began with Reynolds, one piano teacher, and nine students. In later years, Reynolds recalled studying late into the night to stay one day ahead of his students.

Reynolds was re-elected to the faculty for 1916-1917, when enrollment grew to 16 music students. By 1919, the school had grown to five faculty members teaching 61 students, and offered a three-year course leading to a Bachelor of Gospel Music. Reynolds carried a near-impossible teaching load—sight reading, elementary and advanced harmony, composition, elementary and advanced conducting, practical church music, music history, history of hymns, tunes and their use, and normal training.

The curriculum attracted devotees, and by 1921, the department, with 15 faculty members and 209 students, became the School of Gospel Music at The Southwestern Baptist Theological Seminary. The addition of the Master of Gospel Music degree followed in 1922.

That year, Fort Worth's first radio station, WBAP, began operation, and Reynolds was eager to utilize this new medium to showcase the seminary. A February 27, 1925, broadcast featured the men's quartet, the Southwestern Four. Weekly programs by Southwestern Seminary faculty and students followed.

Reynolds also began the beloved annual tradition of a Christmas performance of G.F. Handel's *Messiah* at Southwestern Seminary. On

Tuesday evening, December 20, 1921, this oratorio was performed by the Choral Club and Orchestra, with Reynolds conducting.

"Years later, students who sang in these performances in the early '20s told of the problems they encountered," his nephew, William J. Reynolds, later wrote. "At times, it seemed as though the choir would dissolve in confusion. Only Reynolds' steady, confident beat kept them going."

The *Messiah* performances became major events. In 1923, the Choral Club was accompanied by the Fort Worth Little Symphony Orchestra. In 1931, the entire work was first presented—a three-hour performance without intermission. The practice of singing the complete oratorio continued each year through 1943, the last *Messiah* performance that Reynolds conducted. Over nearly a century, performances have been held at both Southwestern Seminary and Bass Performance Hall, and in November 2019, the School of Church Music and Worship delivered its 98th *Messiah* performance.

The School of Gospel Music initially shared a building with the School of Theology, but with growth, separate quarters were needed. A gift of $150,000 from Mrs. George E. Cowden was designated for a music building honoring her late husband, a Southwestern Seminary trustee. When Scarborough came to Reynolds' office to report the gift, he asked Reynolds to begin making plans for the building. Reynolds reached into his desk drawer and handed Scarborough the plans he had completed two years earlier—plans for a three-story building with curving staircases. When Cowden Hall was completed in 1926, the newly named School of Sacred Music reflected an expanding curriculum.

Unfortunately, this era of expansion was brought to an end by the Great Depression of the 1930s. Salaries were halved. Half of that was paid in money, and the rest in shares of Rio Grande Valley citrus land that had been gifted to the seminary. After a freeze, however, all the trees died.

When the music faculty was reduced, Reynolds offered his resignation rather than ask one of his teachers to leave. After learning what Reynolds had done, three other faculty members offered to be the one to leave instead. One of these was B.B. McKinney, a popular evangelistic singer. Reluctantly, President Scarborough accepted McKinney's resignation because, of the four men, he had the greatest prospect of surviving financially. Later, some speculated that Reynolds had fired McKinney, but their enduring friendship disputed this.

Reynolds continued to contribute to the body of church music. He composed two sacred music dramas, four cantatas, and miscellaneous hymns and Gospel songs. In 1942, the Southern School of Fine Arts in Houston awarded him an honorary Doctor of Music degree.

In the fall of 1944, Reynolds became ill, suffering from hypertension. The following year, after 30 years as head of the music school, he retired. He made Fort Worth his home until his death on May 10, 1949. At his memorial service on the seminary campus, Cowden Hall brimmed with former students and friends.

With the appointment of Ellis L. Carnett as Reynolds' successor, a new era of church music dawned. Southern Baptist churches began rising to the challenge of leading congregations in new ways through musical ministry, expanding a trail first blazed by I.E. Reynolds.

- Julie Owens

J.M. PRICE

J.M. Price was nearing the end of his Master of Theology program in Kentucky when he received a letter from L.R. Scarborough, the new president of the young Southwestern Baptist Theological Seminary. Scarborough had written to offer Price a professorship at the seminary, and he outlined a vision for the seminary's endeavors in the area of Christian education and pedagogy. Scarborough was looking for a pioneer who had the drive and vision to establish a school unlike any other.

"It is now our purpose to establish a School of Christian Pedagogy," Scarborough wrote. "I think we have hold of the small end of a big proposition. We will have to do pioneer work and break new ground."

"As I understand it," Scarborough continued, "this school of pedagogy will be a rare thing in this country, the only one in the South and even beyond the South. The Sunday School Board men are very enthusiastic about this movement and believe that it is one of the most distinctive and far-reaching Kingdom matters started within many years."

Price carefully considered the offer. He had already envisioned popularizing Bible study among the masses, and he wanted religious education to be not just for pastors, but for Sunday School teachers, laymen, and everyday church members. Price envisioned rural farmers, mothers, and laborers who knew why they believed what they believed, and were trained to teach that knowledge to others.

Although a monumental assignment lay before him, Price believed it was the beginning of the life work to which God had called him. His move to Fort Worth, Texas, would set into motion his groundbreaking work at Southwestern Seminary for both the institution and the broader

Southern Baptist Convention. His list of accomplishments and "firsts" are evidence of a visionary-pioneer leader and educator who would have a lasting impact on how churches promoted the Kingdom of God.

John Milburn Price was born on November 21, 1884, on a farm near Fair Dealing, Kentucky. The youngest of eight children, Price was named after the prominent preacher J.H. Milburn, a visiting preacher whose sermon ultimately led Price's mother, Elizabeth, to give her life to the Lord.

Price's parents were both great influences in his life, responsible for many of the characteristics that made him the great leader he was. Many would attest that, like his mother, Price's tenacity and determination were central to his success in a pioneering task.

Even at a young age, Price had a deep respect for Sunday School and the way in which it could influence students. The role of teacher held immeasurable possibilities. He often said that he considered Sunday School teachers to be "the greatest force for good in the nation."

At the age of 18, Price began teaching at a school near the Price farm, teaching 37 pupils in wide-ranging subjects and grade levels. During that time, he also began studies for the undergraduate degree he would complete in 1905 at the age of 20.

Price's ministry eventually led him to Southwestern Seminary, where he had been called upon to build a school of religious education from the ground up.

Price joined the seminary faculty in 1915 and hit the ground running. But the task did not prove easy at first. When the other new professor, I.E. Reynolds, shared with Price his enrollment numbers for the new music program, Price became discouraged.

People seemed eager to join the new music program, but Price had only two students in the education program. Enrollment numbers were an indication of the novelty of such a program—there was little for Price to model in this area of study.

At the time, the only other school of religious pedagogy in the country was in Hartford, Connecticut, but the Hartford school had no denominational association, and Price wanted to train Baptists to do work in Baptist churches. Other seminaries offered single courses in pedagogies, but they primarily existed to train pastors.

Additionally, churches were not yet looking for educational leaders in their churches and staffs. In 1915, only four Southern Baptist churches had educational workers.

Even still, Price set out to create a curriculum that, while beneficial for pastors, would train other men and women for their purposes in the church.

As Price reflected on the task before him, he said, "All former experience in training for religious education must go on the scrap heap. My school must be on a bigger and better scale. I might as well face it: I must blaze a new trail in religious education."

With a newly established religious education curriculum and a newly hired faculty, the education department saw steady growth in its first few years. In 1919, its first graduate, Lou Ella Austin, received a diploma in religious education.

That same year, Price made more pioneering steps at Southwestern Seminary. He created age-specific courses, including elementary, adolescent, and adult religious education. Additionally, students admitted to the Doctor of Theology program were allowed to major in religious education.

By 1920, student enrollment in the new school had increased to 121 students from 16 states. Price had established a three-year curriculum that would lead to the Master of Religious Education, and he began to hire more experienced faculty in their respective fields.

Price established many more "firsts," including the creation of departments devoted to more specific disciplines such as principles of religious education, administration, and church efficiency.

Every decision Price made was groundbreaking simply for its novelty. No other seminary had devoted such time and resources to religious education, offering practical field study while maintaining the academic rigor expected of a theological education.

With an evolving School of Religious Education, more churches began to see the results from this pioneering work. They began to hire educational ministers and put an emphasis on their Sunday School programs. Churches built new structures with this in mind, allowing for more classroom space than ever before.

As early as 1925, Price wanted a building to house the School of Religious Education. Price even had sketches drawn for the vision. It would be another 20 years before that would be set into motion, but he was patient and persistent.

At the time of the proposed construction of the Memorial Building in the early 1940s, Price was determined to also see the construction of the education building. Due to his diligence, the project was approved, and Price spearheaded the fundraising efforts for the building.

Finally, in 1949, the long-awaited building was opened and named in honor of the school's founder and leader. Price Hall was the first of its kind. No other institution had constructed a building for the purpose of training laymen, Sunday School teachers, and ministers of education.

Although such educational programs and ministry focuses were nearly nonexistent at the beginning of the 20th century, they soon became the standard thanks to Price and the work he did at Southwestern Seminary. The demand quickly outpaced the rate at which the seminary could train students. Even pastors, who had otherwise been skeptical of these programs, were convinced of the need to take classes in religious education to better lead the laymen of their congregations.

When Price retired in 1956 at the age of 71, he had served under presidents L.R. Scarborough, E.D. Head, and J. Howard Williams. He had led the School of Religious Education for 41 years, teaching longer than any other Southwestern Seminary professor at the time. In a two-page spread of the 1956 issue of Southwestern News, a list of all his accomplishments and "firsts" outlined the story of a man who pioneered a new trail in theological and religious education at Southwestern Seminary, the SBC, and even other religious institutions. Some of these "firsts" included: first in America to offer a religious education diploma (1917); first in requiring supervised fieldwork as a requirement for a degree (1920); and first school of religious education among Southern Baptists to be accredited (1951).

Even after retirement, Price held the title of director emeritus of the school and retained his office in Price Hall, where he continued writing, studying, and counseling students and professors in their work. To the end of his life, he remained determined to see generations trained for their individual callings.

After recounting stories and experiences with Price, one former student concluded, "I hope we remember the principles and methods he taught us as well as we remember his stories. I suppose he has trained more educational directors than any other man, living or dead."

By the time Price retired, many men and women had graduated from his pioneer program, adopted his ideas and methods, and were making it their life's work to blaze new trails in their own churches for the glory of Christ and to further the Kingdom of God.

- Katie Coleman

T.B. MASTON

During a weeklong revival at a small Tennessee church, 17-year-old T.B. Maston begrudgingly attended the final evening service. After the preacher delivered his sermon and the church began to sing "Just As I Am," Maston was overwhelmed with emotion and wept in his pew.

A friend placed his arm around Maston to console him. Maston said to him, "I wish I could accept the pastor's invitation."

The friend simply replied, "You can if you will."

Later recalling his moment of salvation, Maston said, "If I interpret it correctly, what happened to me that night was that back behind those pews in the old Smithwood church, I said, 'I will'; and when one says, 'I will' to God, he surrenders his will to the Lord's will."

For the remainder of his life, Maston would make that daily decision to surrender to the Lord's will.

Thomas Buford Maston was a highly regarded teacher and ethicist. He became a pioneer in ethics at The Southwestern Baptist Theological Seminary, and was particularly known for the way in which he influenced the Southern Baptist Convention's thoughts on race.

Maston made a profound cultural impact as an ethicist, but his first love was his calling as a teacher.

Not long after his salvation, Maston sensed a call to ministry. He was confident in this call and willing to surrender to the Lord's will, but he struggled for many years to discern the specifics of this calling.

Maston never felt at ease with the idea of being a pastor. In fact, he later made it a point to serve the church as a layman rather than as an ordained minister.

In the meantime, Maston started teaching Sunday School classes and served as the occasional fill-in for Sunday sermons. Through such opportunities, he discovered not only an aptitude for teaching, but a calling from the Lord.

He went on to graduate from Carson-Newman College in Tennessee in 1920, where he met his wife, Essie Mae McDonald. Each of them was eager in pursuing God's calling on their lives, so both enrolled in Southwestern Seminary in the fall of 1920, completing their Master of Religious Education degrees in 1923.

Maston went on to pursue a Doctor of Religious Education, the first student to do so at Southwestern Seminary, as well as additional degrees from Texas Christian University (M.A. Sociology, 1927) and Yale University (Ph.D. in Christian Ethics, 1939).

Maston began teaching at Southwestern Seminary in 1922, and in the following years established a robust Christian ethics curriculum. In 1943, he crafted a department of Christian social ethics at the seminary.

As a teacher, Maston prioritized relationships with students and was devoted to daily prayer for them. He was a favorite for many seminary students, both as a teacher and mentor. Maston once said of his calling to teach, "I'd rather teach than eat. I've never taught a class that I didn't enjoy."

Maston taught during the Civil Rights movement, when people were calling for justice, even within the church. He emerged as an influential figure at Southwestern Seminary and in the SBC for how he taught others to look at social issues through a biblical lens.

Occasionally, his commitment to Scripture put him at odds with people, particularly regarding race. He led many in the denomination to face their sin of racism and to recognize that the treatment of minority groups had not been based on Christian ethics and biblical principles.

Maston was passionate about whatever he taught and was willing to push back on old ways that did not align with the Bible, yet he always did so with kindness and compassion. He received many supportive letters during those years, but he received equally as many letters condemning his work that advocated for a racially inclusive denomination.

In an address to the SBC in the early 1950s, Maston pled with

Southern Baptists to not be on the wrong side of history regarding race and the Supreme Court's recent decision to declare segregation in the schools unconstitutional. The speech garnered national attention and was reported by both religious and secular publications.

Maston's work as an ethicist made him a much sought-after figure in denominational service and in community roles. He hepled form the SBC Christian Life Commission (now known as the Ethics and Religious Libery Commission) along with J. Howard Williams and others; served on SBC advisory councils; and served in community organizations including the National Association for the Advancement of Colored People and the Local Urban League.

Maston taught on race in five of the Southern Baptist seminaries and, by 1938, began to offer a new course, "Social Problems of the South." Then, in 1944, he offered a course entirely devoted to race, "The Church and The Race Problem."

In this latter course, Maston asked black leaders to address the class and frequently took students to Fort Worth black communities. "I always thought that the trips would be the things they would remember the most about the course," Maston said. He also required student field study and reports on a selected social problem in Fort Worth, such as provision for blacks in the public school system.

After one meeting with black leaders in North Texas during which Maston spoke about love, one man asked him, "Isn't there a real danger that one may make love a substitute for justice, a mere sentimentality?"

Maston answered, "Not genuine Christian love. It is inclusive of justice."

In 1951, Southwestern Seminary opened regular classes to black students, something Maston had urged the seminary to do for many years. One of these students, Clarence Lucas, said of Maston: "At a time when I wasn't even allowed to live in dormitories, Maston would come and talk with me. He offered some direction, and then let me as a proud human being struggle with it myself. I personally prefer this to any paternalism."

Although progress was made in the broader culture and in the SBC,

Maston recognized that such accomplishments did not call for self-congratulation, but rather pointed to the need to keep pressing on in the difficult but necessary work.

Racism and its effects were not settled; rather, "There are plenty of things that still need to be done," Maston said.

Maston retired from his teaching position at Southwestern Seminary in May 1963, but he continued to follow the Lord's will for his life. He retained his seminary office, where he continued to meet with students, study, and devote time to writing. In fact, Maston published more works in retirement than in the entirety of his career.

Of his many articles and books, some of his noteworthy publications include *Segregation and Desegregation* and *The Bible and Race*, both of which are considered widely significant contributions on race.

Maston's influence was far-reaching, but possibly the most significant way in which he impacted the denomination was through the generations of students he taught who also surrendered to the Lord's will, faithfully served in churches and on the mission field, and led Southern Baptists to honor the Lord in their own callings.

– Katie Coleman

FLOY BARNARD

As an inquisitive and thoughtful teenager, Floy Barnard knew she had been called to educational ministry. For nearly three decades, this remarkably bright young woman made her light shine at The Southwestern Baptist Theological Seminary in service to young women seeking to study God's Word. Standing for 104 years, Barnard Hall remains a tribute to her service.

Florence M. "Floy" Barnard was born July 8, 1895, in Dawkins Pueblo, Colorado, to Jehu Kimbo Barnard and Mary Ann Barnard. An alumna of Colorado College of Education with Bachelor of Arts and Master of Arts degrees, she graduated twice from Southwestern Seminary, first with a Master of Religious Education in 1929 and then with a Doctor of Religious Education in 1939. While a seminary student, she served several churches in Fort Worth as an educational director. In 1957, the University of Mary Hardin-Baylor in Belton awarded her the honorary Doctor of Literature degree. She served as a trustee at Mary Hardin-Baylor from 1957-1960.

But Barnard was more than just a string of scholastic titles and degrees earned. Throughout her career, the selfless educator willingly shared her talents, time, and knowledge, taking young female seminary students under her wing to guide them to their own academic successes, and endearing herself to them and to the seminary in the process.

Barnard joined the Southwestern Seminary faculty in 1933 during the heart of the Great Depression to teach missionary education and educational arts in the department of religious education. Though the seminary, hit hard by the stock market crash, had begun slashing faculty salaries in half in 1929, Barnard was among the faithful who remained on staff during those difficult years.

Diversity in course offerings was essential then because of the reduction in the number of teachers employed. To help meet the needs of students, Barnard combined and taught an array of courses. She also developed courses in religious dramatics, a discipline that would hold a major place in future curriculum development. Later, she served as a committee member of the Southern Baptist Convention's Film Commission.

While at Southwestern Seminary, Barnard was a popular conference leader and speaker throughout the SBC. Beginning in 1935, she spoke annually at the Ridgecrest and Glorieta Baptist conference centers and was active in the SBC's Woman's Missionary Union.

Coming out of the Depression, the seminary hummed with a new sense of missionary zeal and an influx of willing students. Barnard remained on the faculty, but her most distinctive contribution to Southwestern Seminary was her contact and influence with hundreds of young women who arrived on campus. She intensified that service as dean of women, beginning with her election to that position in 1942 and continuing until her retirement 18 years later.

As director of the women's dormitory, Barnard served as counselor, friend, house mother, and confidant to the young women under her guidance. Her influence was so great that trustees named the women's dormitory Floy Barnard Hall in 1960 "because of her gracious spirit and total dedication that had so endeared her" to the seminary and its women.

"The girls have contributed to me more than I ever have to them," Barnard wrote. "I would say that positively they are the most wonderful girls in the world."

During President Robert Naylor's administration at Southwestern Seminary, the School of Religious Education was one of four that experienced significant growth, and numerous faculty were added to meet teaching needs. It was during this period that Barnard retired after spring graduation in 1960, at age 65. Trustees moved then to name the women's dormitory for her.

Like its namesake, Barnard Hall has a storied history, having served many purposes dating back to its construction in 1914. Southwestern Seminary had already been training both men and women since the school was established in 1908, but after the seminary's relocation to Fort Worth in 1910, plans were made to construct a building that would house the Women's Missionary Training School. When the building opened in 1915, it provided a space uniquely devoted to training the seminary's female students who had answered the call to a life of ministry and service. Trustees found Floy Barnard to be a natural choice to guide these young women.

Like Floy Barnard herself, Barnard Hall served endless numbers of female students. It is still the official residence for women on the Southwestern Seminary campus and is Southwestern Seminary's second oldest structure (after Fort Worth Hall).

Serving tirelessly throughout her Southwestern Seminary tenure, Barnard was also known for her contribution to many areas of denominational life, leadership, and teaching. She was active in the SBC's Woman's Missionary Union and contributed to many written works, including Sunday School lessons for the Baptist Sunday School Board.

She authored two books—*Drama in the Churches* and *Christian Witnessing*—and four Bible study books. While she was an inspirational speaker at many conventions worldwide, she continued to say that she found her greatest joy in serving at Southwestern Seminary. In 1967, Barnard was one of three recipients of Southwestern Seminary's Distinguished Alumni award.

After her retirement, Barnard continued to teach the Word of God. She led conferences at mission field meetings in Argentina, Brazil, Chile, Mexico, and Guatemala until her death in 1992, in Sunnyvale, California.

– Julie Owens

E.D. HEAD

Eleven-year-old E.D. Head felt his father's strong embrace and his bearded cheek pressed against his own as his father poignantly whispered, "I'm glad you surrendered to Christ tonight."

His father had perfectly stated what the young E.D. Head had just done on this spring evening in 1903. Convicted during a revival service in Arcadia, Louisiana, the eventual third president of The Southwestern Baptist Theological Seminary had given his life to the Lord in unconditional surrender. From then on, the driving force of his life became: "What does God want me to do?"

What followed was a life characterized by obedience, faith, and godliness. As a pastor, evangelist, author, professor, seminary president, and man of God, Head obeyed the Lord's call, trusted Him with a sincere faith, and sought to love his neighbors with selfless compassion. In so doing, he ushered Southwestern Seminary into a new phase of its history, keeping the fires of its founding fathers alive while promoting faith and trust in the Lord during a time of unprecedented enrollment and financial security.

Eldred Douglas Head was born in 1892 in Sparta, Louisiana. Following his profession of faith in Christ at the age of 11, Head became an ardent preacher-evangelist, sharing written sermons with friends, leading prayer meetings in the park, and preaching to all who would listen from a cotton gin or in the woods.

"From the beginning of my Christian experience, there was nothing for me but the ministry," he said.

Head earned bachelor's and master's degrees from Baylor University and a Master of Theology and Doctor of Theology from Southwestern

Seminary. He proceeded to teach at Baylor in such subjects as Old and New Testament survey, the life and literature of Paul, and missions and evangelism. He also pastored multiple churches in Texas, including the First Baptist Church of Houston from 1932-1942.

In his first sermon at FBC Houston in September 1932, Head provided a glimpse of his heart for the Lord, for which he would later become well-known. Preaching on Genesis 22:18, Head shared that "the way of peace, joy, and happy fellowship is the way of obedience to God's voice."

Such obedience would lead Head to resign from his pastorate 10 years later in order to succeed L.R. Scarborough as the third president of Southwestern Seminary. Head made this resignation with some reluctance, having greatly enjoyed shepherding his congregation, but he nevertheless sensed that God's call was clear.

"I have never felt for one moment that I was capable of serving as president of Southwestern," Head later said. "All I have done is to follow the path of God's leading."

Head's first meeting with the faculty as president took place on July 3, 1942. Though little was done in the way of business, L.R. Elliott, secretary of the faculty, recollected, "[Dr. Head's] friendliness, humility, religious earnestness, skill in presiding, and his vision won the hearts of all present."

During his inaugural address later that year, Head affirmed his pastoral heart and Kingdom focus, declaring, "Let me summon every one of you, redeemed by the blood of Christ, impassioned with a holy urge, to evangelistic conquest—committed wholly to the infallible and unimpeachable Word of God; devoted to the patronage of the highest scholarship, to His riven side, His cross of atoning sacrifice."

"God helping us, we will not fail this beloved seminary," he continued—"neither those who have gone on before us, nor our glorious denomination which trusts us, nor this broken, disillusioned world so sorely in need of the anchorage which can be found only in Him who can never fail, even Jesus Christ our Lord."

Head's 11-year presidency saw great advancements in the life of the seminary. He began his tenure at the tail end of the Great Depression, when the entire country had returned to economic prosperity following the outbreak of World War II. So, in just his second year as president, Head announced to the Faculty Council that the seminary had funds to pay off its debt. A thanksgiving service was held in November 1943, and former president L.R. Scarborough was invited to burn the final note.

Head also promptly began the process of restoring faculty and staff salaries to their pre-Depression levels. As inflationary trends increased, Head made this an item of discussion among trustees nearly every year. In a similar manner, he made efforts to restore and repair student housing in Fort Worth Hall and Barnard Hall.

These renovations were more important than ever due to the enormous increase in the size of the student body between 1942 and 1953. Enrollment in the former was 734; by 1953, it had grown to 2,160, an increase of more than 180 percent.

Acknowledging this immense growth, Head reported to the Southern Baptist Convention one year that the professors lectured not to classes, but to "congregations." This increased enrollment was certainly encouraging, says historian Robert A. Baker, but it "strained to the limit the ability of the school to assimilate a large number of new students from widely divergent backgrounds and training."

One means of keeping up with the growing enrollment was the addition of new faculty. In Head's 11-year presidency, the faculty grew from 23 to 42 full-time members, an increase of roughly 83 percent.

Furthermore, Southwestern Seminary built two new buildings during Head's tenure: the B.H. Carroll Memorial Building, which housed, among other things, classrooms, the seminary's library, and a new chapel auditorium; and Price Hall, which would house the School of Religious Education.

When plans for these buildings were first announced, Head declared, "The epic history of Southwestern reveals the guiding hand of God from its very beginning to its victorious present. Under the spell of this vision so splendid, let us dedicate ourselves and our resources unto its complete realization."

Two years later, as construction of the buildings neared completion, Head, in similar manner, reported to the SBC, "But whatever the achievements and successes, trials or defeats, may this institution never lose sight of Him whose providence made it possible and whose hand now guides its destinies."

Maintaining his focus on people over the institution itself, Head continued, "With all our building, may the buildings never become bigger than the professors or the students. May we never go up on masonry and down on manhood or true intellectuality and spirituality."

Beyond these large-scale developments in the life of the seminary, Head also worked in less visible ways. For example, as Baker states, he "began the orderly transition from the somewhat informal administration of the school to the development of a well-structured body of trustees and a more efficiently organized faculty." Furthermore, reflecting his compassionate heart, he made efforts to recognize the contributions of those who rarely saw the spotlight.

In 1948-1949, for example, the Southwestern News magazine carried a series of brief articles on six administrative staff members, some of whom had served since the early 1910s, including the school's nursery supervisor and the bookkeeper for the business office. Head personally wrote these articles, Baker says, "reflecting the kind of gracious and thoughtful spirit that characterized him."

Head also occupied the Chair of Evangelism, or "Chair of Fire," during his presidency. Across his first eight years at the seminary, he taught thousands of students in the classroom, encouraging a fresh zeal for evangelism. In 1950, Head stepped back from teaching responsibilities in order to focus more fully on administrative matters, but he continued to produce scholarly resources for students, including a revision of Scarborough's *With Christ After the Lost*, which provided instruction and encouragement for the evangelistic task.

After suffering a heart attack late in his presidency, Head received the news that he would be bed-ridden for weeks and out of the pulpit for a year. Displaying his steadfast faith, Head tapped his chest and said to a friend, "I have no doubt but that somehow this is in God's plan, and I still believe in Romans 8:28."

Though Head eventually returned to his responsibilities, he soon sensed that just as the Lord had called him to resign the pastorate and assume the presidency, so now the Lord was calling him to step down from Southwestern Seminary. Head resigned after the spring 1953 semester, assuring his final graduating class of his confidence "that the Lord who has always led and revealed His will, will still lead on and make known His will."

Ray Summers, then a professor at Southwestern Seminary and a close personal friend of Head, noted that such a sentiment was common for this man of God, perfectly encapsulating the driving force of his obedient, faithful, and godly life. This was further reinforced by a quotation on the flyleaf of Head's Bible: "What is it that God keeps on bringing before you? Obey the vision! Perform the duty! Keep the commandment! Make the sacrifice! He who keeps the vision gets greater ability to see, and he who refuses increases his blindness."

Head eventually regained his health, and in ongoing surrender to God's call, he spent the rest of his life preaching, teaching, and writing. Until the death of this compassionate, godly man in 1964, "there was nothing for [him] but the ministry."

- Alex Sibley

J. HOWARD WILLIAMS

During the summer of 1903, seemingly all Dallas children were going to the circus that had come to town. All children, that is, except for 9-year-old J. Howard Williams and his brothers. Although they were eager to go to the circus like their peers, their father encouraged the young boys to stay home and work on the family's small acreage of cotton. He did so, he told them, not out of punishment, but for a bigger purpose.

The following Sunday, a special offering was to be taken for foreign missions, and Mr. Williams wanted his family to have something to offer.

"Boys, let's pick all the cotton we can and give it to missions," Mr. Williams said. "This will take the Gospel to little children who have never heard the Word."

The Williams family sacrificed a day at the circus and instead put all their time and energy into doing their part for missions, something that forever impacted the life and eventual ministry of J. Howard Williams.

Williams would become a visionary leader and a passionate evangelist, and nearly everything he did was in service of winning souls. He took on many roles before ultimately becoming The Southwestern Baptist Theological Seminary's fourth president, where he carried out a vision for training men and women for ministry. Although he was only able to serve Southwestern Seminary for five years before his death, in those short years, he was able to accomplish an extraordinary amount of work.

John Howard Williams was born near Dallas on July 3, 1894. His parents were some of his greatest spiritual influences, but he also had the privilege of hearing the teachings of one of the greatest preachers of his day: George W. Truett.

In his childhood and teenage years, Williams frequently attended Sunday School at the First Baptist Church of Dallas and eventually joined in membership with his family.

After hearing a message preached by Truett during a 1902 revival meeting, Williams placed his faith in Jesus Christ. He privately confessed his faith to his mother at home, but his father wanted both Williams and his brother to receive spiritual counsel from Truett.

Before the revival week concluded, Mr. Williams took the boys to meet with Truett. Finally, Truett said to Mr. Williams, "I think these boys know what they are doing, and they want to make a public profession of faith. I believe they are ready. I have questioned them thoroughly."

Williams continued to grow in his faith in the following years and eventually sensed the Lord calling him to preach at age 16. An influential figure in this call was Brother Waldron, who worked in the Dallas Rescue Mission.

Williams had been a regular worker at the Mission, coming daily to assist in whatever way he could. After having spent time with the young Williams, one day, Waldron finally said, "Young man, isn't the Lord calling you to preach?"

"Oh, no, Brother Waldron! Surely He couldn't use me as a preacher," Williams said. "I have no education, no training, and nothing to offer the Lord."

Having dropped out of school after the fourth grade due to an eye condition, Williams had doubts about his ability to become an effective preacher. Waldron let the matter rest for some time, but later pressed the issue again.

Williams finally admitted that despite his insecurities and the obstacles before him, "I had rather preach than do anything on earth. … I am ready to begin."

Williams quickly seized every preaching opportunity, including at the Mission where he eventually took charge at the request of the Dallas Baptist Association. The Mission later became a church, which Williams pastored until 1920 when he was called to a church in Venus, Texas.

During this time, Williams enrolled in classes at Southwestern Seminary (he previously took night classes before earning his bachelor's degree at Baylor University) and met his wife, Floy Kelley, another enthusiastic soul-winner with aspirations of becoming a missionary.

Williams was a well-regarded pastor of seven Southern Baptist churches. He exemplified all the best characteristics of a preacher, leader, and shepherd. One of his church members said of him, "Shepherding was probably one of Dr. Williams' strongest points as a pastor. He was so gracious and understanding that everyone looked forward to a visit with him."

In each church, Williams strengthened the organizational structure and created opportunities for the training and equipping of its members to be ministers of the Gospel. Williams did groundbreaking work in each of his churches, creating new staff positions and establishing religious education programs, for example.

Another church member said of him, "He always had plans and goals to set before the people and knew how to challenge them to achieve those goals."

Williams always had a large vision for what the church could be, and a larger vision for how that work could impact the Kingdom of God. This visionary leadership made him the perfect fit to lead a new era of Southwestern Seminary.

But long before he became the seminary's president, Williams and his wife met with the retired president L.R. Scarborough in 1945. In that meeting, Scarborough said he believed God would someday call Williams to be Southwestern Seminary's president.

Surprised by the suggestion, Williams replied, "Dr. Scarborough, I am not a school man. I am hardly qualified for that work."

But Scarborough simply replied, "Howard, do not limit God!"

Eight years later, the seminary was searching for another president and had nominated Williams as their choice candidate. By then, Williams was well-experienced in denominational and administrative work, having served as executive secretary and president of the Baptist General Convention of Texas. Even so, Williams was hesitant at first to assume the presidency. But after much prayer, he eventually accepted the task and took office on August 1, 1953, becoming the fourth president of Southwestern Seminary.

In his inaugural address, Williams laid out a vision for the seminary. He had three essential goals for his presidency—enlarge the faculty, update campus facilities, and increase the endowment. The seminary had seen much growth in recent years as it neared its fiftieth anniversary. Significant growth required a significant vision for the future. Williams was the man for the job.

"I always knew when he was 'hatching' a dream," Mrs. Williams said of her husband's work. "It spilled over and ran all over the place. He would say to a guest in the home, 'Get in the car. I want to show you something.' He would then take the guest to the spot on or near the campus where he had by faith seen in his mind the building that was needed there."

During Williams' presidency, the seminary saw unprecedented growth. Enrollment numbers dramatically increased, Williams made 37 additions to the teaching staff, and he set into motion plans for updated facilities, technologies, and library resources.

Although Williams was not able to see the entirety of his vision fulfilled before he died on April 20, 1958, he was able to see many of those remaining goals set into motion, including additional student housing north of the campus, which was eventually named in his honor.

Despite his previous concern that he was not a "school man," Williams quickly adapted. But he also recognized where he had shortcomings and often called faculty and other individuals to his office for advice and counsel.

This humility was beneficial to the seminary's success, as well as to the relationship between president and employee. Williams was viewed as a trusted friend and colleague devoted to serving the Kingdom of God.

In a 1955 editorial in the Southwestern News magazine, Williams wrote of his high regard for the Southwestern Seminary faculty:

"Now that I am well into my second year with Southwestern, I can say that my admiration of and affection for the faculty have increased with the passing months. I like them as men and women who are agreeable to work with. I like them as a team cooperating in a united effort. I admire them as Christian men and women who are dedicated to the high calling of teaching.

"… The dedication of the faculty to the Lord, to Southwestern, and to the high calling of teacher is further evidenced by the fact that many of them stay here even though they are sought for in other fields of service."

Even with all of his many titles and accomplishments, Williams' primary objective was to win souls to Christ. The role of evangelist was such a natural part of his character that he could not help but share Christ with every person he met in any situation.

"How are you getting along, neighbor?" was a common phrase to hear from Williams at any given time just before he inquired about the individual's salvation.

E.W. Jackson, a church layman, noted that Williams was "the most consistent man in this area that I have ever known." There was no meeting that could not be delayed, no appointment too important that he would not stop to share with the taxi driver, restaurant server, or the general passerby.

His passion and care for the souls of all people inspired his students, staff, and faculty. Southwestern Seminary was in a time of academic flourishing and administrative growth, but by his leadership, soul-winning remained one of the seminary's primary passions.

Reflecting on the life and work of J. Howard Williams, pastor W.A. Criswell said, "He had the heart of a pastor, and in whatever capacity he served our Lord, either as an executive in the denomination or as a president of one of our schools, he was ever the shepherd and the guardian of the flock."

– Katie Coleman

ROBERT E. NAYLOR

In his 1958 inaugural address, Robert E. Naylor posed the question, "Is there a single word that can tie together the first year of the seminary's life with this year and the last year?"

In The Southwestern Baptist Theological Seminary's first 50 years, much had changed from the time of B.H. Carroll and the seminary's founding faculty. L.R. Scarborough, E.D. Head, and J. Howard Williams were worthy successors who led the seminary through many challenges and triumphs. Each had a unique vision for the seminary, and even while changes naturally occurred in that time, there remained one constant.

"The word is *Gospel*," Naylor concluded.

As he addressed the men and women of Southwestern Seminary and the Southern Baptist Convention, Naylor ushered in a new era, the beginning of another 50 years of God-called men and women trained to be ministers of the Gospel.

Robert Naylor continued a legacy of Gospel devotion at the seminary with which he had a long relationship as student, friend, trustee, and president. Throughout his 20-year presidency, Naylor cast and executed a vision for a thriving institution that would emerge as the largest seminary in the world.

In his inaugural address, Naylor called for a "Gospel fellowship" of individuals who would surrender to God as "Gospel preachers, teachers, students, and witnesses." He continued, "The meaning of our ministries and the unity of our diversity is the Gospel."

First addressing students, Naylor said, "The student in the seminary says, 'I have believed. Therefore, by the will and special call of God, I must preach the Gospel.' So this one turns away from a professional study to the seminary. This one turns away with his engineering degree to the things of theology. The compulsion becomes primary in life."

As a young man, Naylor had also abandoned pursuit of another career for the calling of preacher of the Gospel.

Born on January 24, 1909, Naylor was the son of a Baptist preacher. Naylor later recounted memories of traveling with his father in a horse-drawn buggy to visit many small congregations in Oklahoma.

Much of his early life revolved around the church, but his sights were set on a future in business. Naylor was a brilliant student who skipped several grades throughout his primary education, eventually completing his college degree before the age of 20.

During his senior year of college at East Central State College in Oklahoma, Naylor surrendered to the Lord's calling and made the dramatic decision to move to Fort Worth, Texas, to attend Southwestern Seminary. Although the 19-year-old did not yet meet the age requirement for admission, he was able to gain special permission from President L.R. Scarborough.

During his second year in the seminary, Naylor started his first position as a part-time pastor of a church in Ada, Oklahoma. He also preached at some other small congregations near the town.

Each weekend, Naylor left his J.C. Penney department store job at 10 p.m., caught the next available train, and slept on the train for the 180-mile ride to Ada, usually arriving around 5 a.m.

Once there, Naylor would preach his first service in Ada, and then make the preaching rounds to about four other congregations throughout the day before catching the 3 a.m. train back to Fort Worth.

Naylor graduated in 1932 with a Master of Theology and soon received his first full-time pastorate. For the following 15 years, this Southwesterner served in several churches in such places as Arkadelphia, Arkansas; Nashville, Arkansas; and Enid, Oklahoma. He eventually returned to Fort Worth in 1952 to pastor Travis Avenue Baptist Church, where he served until 1958.

During those years, Naylor also began serving many institutions' committees and trustee boards. In 1941, nine years after his graduation from the seminary, Naylor became a member of Southwestern Seminary's board of trustees. He served during the presidencies of E.D. Head and J. Howard Williams. He chaired several committees and was twice elected board chairman.

Naylor treasured these years and the opportunity to serve his alma mater. In his inaugural address, he noted the significant role trustees, as well as other supporting roles, played in the seminary's success.

"The layman, the trustee, the friend of the institution, says, 'Having believed, I must help in training the called of God. I will give direction and advice, build a building, give money to endow a chair of teaching in this institution, preach the Gospel through thousands of lives.'"

In 1958, Southwestern Seminary mourned the sudden loss of their president, J. Howard Williams. He had set into motion many plans and visions for the school, but was unable to complete many of them before his death. Upon his nomination to the presidency, Naylor took up the mantle and began to lead the seminary into a new era, promising to lead his beloved seminary with a commitment to the past while marching forward toward a bright future.

Among the seminary's founding principles was a devotion to missions and evangelism. Naylor reaffirmed these principles and promised a presidency devoted to the Gospel and to the Word of God.

In his inaugural address, Naylor continued, "The administration says, 'I have believed [the Gospel]. Therefore, under His will, I must lead in training the ministers, sending missionaries, building a school, dreaming dreams.'"

Naylor had many dreams for the future, and he saw many of those dreams come to fruition as enrollment numbers swelled to an all-time high, making Southwestern Seminary the largest seminary in the world at that time.

Due to the dramatic growth in those 20 years, the seminary required many additions and updates. As early as 1959, Naylor began making additions to the faculty, ultimately doubling the number of professors by 1978.

Naylor was a man of great conviction, particularly regarding what he described as the Christian's duty to evangelism and to the Word of God, a high standard he had for himself and his faculty. Addressing such a role in his inaugural address, he said, "The teacher says, 'I have believed the Gospel. Therefore I must teach the Gospel in the seminary.' Teaching is more than a profession or vocation; it is the handling of the Word of life."

Many of Naylor's chapel sermons, as well as editorials written in Southwestern News, frequently emphasized such principles. No one ever doubted his devotion to the Bible as the "inspired revelation of God."

Southwestern Seminary was also functioning in a new era for seminary funding. The SBC Cooperative Program (CP) had implemented a new funding concept for its six seminaries, an idea for which Naylor himself had advocated. Distribution of CP resources would be reevaluated many more times, but the changes marked the beginning of a new era for SBC theological education and the denominational commitment to supporting seminary men and women.

"The denomination says, 'Our fellowship of faith and cooperation demands that we must train these men and women called of God to preach. These 30,000 new preaching stations will have for them men and women whom God has chosen. These we must train,'" Naylor said.

Through generous donations and especially through new Cooperative Program funds, the seminary was able to fund many projects and necessary campus updates, boost overall operations, renovate existing buildings, and build new structures.

Naylor continued many of his predecessor's campus expansion initiatives, but also launched many new ones. Among the newly envisioned structures completed during his presidency were the Naylor Student Center (which trustees voted to name in his honor), a medical center, an official home for the president, a children's center, and finally a physical fitness center.

On November 22, 1976, Naylor informed the seminary trustees of his plans to retire in two years. He wanted to make the transition a time of ease for his successor. On August 1, 1978, Naylor assumed the title president emeritus, and although he had retired, he continued to be a constant supporter and encourager of the seminary for which he had devoted the majority of his life since leaving his Oklahoma home in pursuit of God's calling at the age of 19.

In his last message to the trustees, Naylor reflected on 20 years of Gospel-devoted service as president of Southwestern Seminary.

"At the outset of this last 20 years," Naylor said, "I made a fresh commitment to my Lord and to the trustees of this seminary that we would faithfully follow Him and that we would adhere to the authoritative revelation of God in Christ Jesus set forth in the One Book. It is on this commitment that I stand, that I ask under God that the years be measured, and that I ask only of Him that I be found faithful."

– Katie Coleman

JOHN EARL SEELIG

As vice president for public affairs, John Seelig served The Southwestern Baptist Theological Seminary with faith and grace for three decades. In leading the seminary to greatness over the years, many men contributed through their teaching, and many through their preaching. But Seelig led Southwestern Seminary to grow exponentially through his gift of amassing vast support from the local community and beyond.

"Those in development work outside the seminary family know Dr. Seelig as the dean of Southern Baptist fundraisers," former Southwestern Seminary president Russell Dilday said of Seelig in 1990.

But though much of his historical significance lies in his tenacity and skill as a seminary vice president, for him, the impact he had on individual lives remained the most significant aspect of his work.

Part of Seelig's responsibilities entailed informing students they would receive scholarships, and he often called them personally to share the news. On one of these phone calls, the wife of a student told Seelig that, due to recently having to quit her job because of complications with her pregnancy, the scholarship was a direct answer to their prayers.

"That's the joy of this job," he reflected. "This is what it's all about."

John Earl Seelig was born in Fredericksburg, Texas, in 1924. After attending high school there, he did undergraduate studies at Hardin-Simmons University, where he was a positive and energetic student and yearbook editor, and he earned a Bachelor of Science degree. In 1947, he married Virginia Garrett, daughter of the late congressman Clyde Garrett.

Virginia Seelig was an accomplished vocalist known for her stirring

Christian performances. Together, the Seeligs were two untiring voices for Christ—hers to praise God in song, his to spread word of the work being done at the seminary for God.

In 1949, Seelig completed a Master of Religious Education degree at Southwestern Seminary, and later received a Doctor of Humanities degree at Hardin-Simmons. He served in area churches and was involved in denominational work until he was hired by then-president Robert Naylor as Southwestern Seminary's vice president for public affairs in 1960. Working in the areas of public relations, fundraising, and alumni affairs, his responsibilities included overseeing all the school's publications (including the Southwestern News magazine), maintaining alumni files, hosting campus visitors, representing the school at conventions, and "all school mimeographing."

During Seelig's tenure, Southwestern Seminary experienced exponential growth. Over his 30 years there, as enrollment doubled, his role grew. He was part of administrative teams that oversaw growth in the seminary endowment from $4.4 million to $46.9 million, budget increases from $1.4 million to $18.5 million, and an increase in assets from $13.6 million to more than $100 million. Physically, the campus added eight buildings.

Still, though, Seelig maintained his focus on people. He initiated the President's Club, the Founders' Circle, the Distinguished Alumni Awards, and the B.H. Carroll Awards. He also restructured the Advisory Council. Though these certainly aimed at strengthening ties with ministry partners and alumni, they also served to honor the individuals who supported the seminary.

"You could not overstate the contribution of John Seelig to the seminary," Naylor said upon Seelig's retirement in 1990. "His sense of personal debt and his creative mind have combined to make up one of the most prolific contributions in the life of this institution."

Dilday added, "Everyone who has any awareness of Southwestern Seminary over the past 30 years knows of the valuable contributions Dr. Seelig has made."

After leaving the seminary, Seelig's passion and focus remained bringing the Word of God to individuals. The Seeligs spent a year in Hawaii serving the Hawaii Baptist Convention; then, after their return to Texas, they became active members of Southcliff Baptist Church. Friends describe Seelig as a loving family man who had a gift for making friends and enjoyed teaching Sunday School at Travis Avenue Baptist Church and Southcliff for a combined 48 years.

Tony Wilford, a member of Southcliff Baptist Church, recalls Seelig's impact on Sunday School groups and his ability to touch the lives of individuals: "I had the privilege of getting to know Dr. Seelig at Southcliff Baptist Church, where he was the Sunday School teacher for my in-laws, Don and Judy Weeks. He was a wonderful man and such an encouragement to me through the years."

For 64 years, Virginia was by her husband's side in his walk with Christ. A voice professor at Southwestern Seminary for 27 years, she was an accomplished contralto soloist with performances ranging from opera and musical theater to oratorios and recitals, to singing with several Billy Graham crusades. She was soloist in a performance of Handel's *Messiah* presented for the King and Queen of Jordan in the Royal Cultural Palace in Amman. In 1988, the seminary's School of Church Music presented her with the Distinguished Service Award.

In honor of the couple's combined 57 years of service for Southwestern Seminary, in 2008, the board of trustees named a room in the Robert E. Naylor Student Center the John and Virginia Seelig Banquet Room. That year, the seminary also honored the Seeligs with the L.R. Scarborough Award.

After Seelig's death in January 2019, many Southwestern Seminary alumni reflected positively on his decades of service. Gerald Hodges, a 1990 Master of Divinity graduate, typified the sentiment: "In 1987, John befriended me and my family when I was a new student at SWBTS. My wife and I both worked in the Registrar's office, where we met Dr. Seelig. He took me to my first rodeo (I am from North Carolina), bought me my first pair of cowboy boots (which I still have), and met me for breakfast regularly, where he offered me great encouragement. I am thankful for his life and love."

– Julie Owens

ROY J. FISH

The last thing Roy Fish said to his students before dismissing class and heading to the airport was, "Make yourself available to God. He wants to use you to touch the life of somebody else." That evening, he shared a similar message with a west Texas church, impressing upon them the importance of witnessing for Christ.

At around 11 o'clock that night, Fish was challenged to practice what he preached. While eating a late dinner at the restaurant of his hotel, he saw a man "with an unusually shaped beard" and thought to himself, "Here is a man with whom I should share." Looking at his watch, however, and seeing that it was nearly midnight, he rejected the thought.

After paying the check, Fish walked into the lobby and found himself advancing toward the man with the beard. Again, he sensed the need to witness to this man, but again, he protested, citing once more the lateness of the hour.

Fish went outside for a breath of fresh air. Upon returning indoors, he stepped onto the elevator, and there, yet again, he found himself in the presence of the man with the beard. Fish seemed to hear God say, "Are you available?"

Reluctantly, Fish removed a pamphlet from his pocket—one produced by the Billy Graham Evangelistic Association. He handed it to the man, who was reading a newspaper, and said, "Here is some good news that you won't read in today's newspaper."

The man took the pamphlet and, seeing Billy Graham's name, revealed that he had once attended one of Graham's evangelistic crusades. "Although he found it stirring," Fish learned, "he left lost, as he had arrived, but hungry to know more. Billy Graham's name on the pamphlet rekindled that hunger."

The next morning, the man accepted Jesus as his Savior. He later became an active member of a Baptist church in New York, sharing his faith with others as Fish had done with him.

Recounting this story in his book *Dare to Share*, Fish said, "Suppose [I] had not been available to God. Then ask yourself this question, 'How many people are there who are just waiting for some available witness to dare to share the Gospel with them?'

"The Holy Spirit is looking for available channels. Will you be one?"

This illustrative experience typifies Fish's life ministry. Since becoming a Christian in his college years and engaging in personal evangelism for the first time soon thereafter, he sought to not only be an available witness for the Lord himself, but also to teach and encourage others to do the same.

"Sharing is to be a part of our constant lifestyle," he said. "Wherever we come in contact with people, the place becomes a potential place of sharing. Anyone with whom we come in contact possibly could be a hurting person—one with whom God would have us share."

Roy Jason Fish was born on February 7, 1930, in Star City, Arkansas. Growing up in church, he was baptized at age 9, but he later realized that he had not truly made a profession of faith, instead thinking that the way to heaven was to join the church, be baptized, and live as good a life as possible. Not until 10 years later, in July 1949, did he finally understand that all of his own efforts toward Christianity had come to nothing; that he had neither deserved nor earned salvation, but could only accept it as Jesus' free gift.

Recalling the words of a hymn sung in church the previous Sunday— "Only Trust Him"—Fish prayed to the Lord, "I trust you as Savior and will trust you to take me to heaven." Fish's life was forever changed.

Later that summer, Fish shared his testimony at a citywide youth revival. The following day, his cousin invited him to join him in visiting some friends from high school and college in order to witness to them. Though nervous to do so, Fish accepted the invitation.

Fish's son, Steve, recalled the experience: "The friends and their families who opened doors at their knocking looked at those Bibles as one might a loaded canon, and it seemed that no one in that particular venture was saved by their witness. However, in a few days, he began to go out alone to see some of his old friends in an effort to win them to Christ. That invitation to go visiting was the beginning of Roy Fish's lifelong practice of telling others about Jesus."

Fish proceeded to serve in his college's Baptist Student Union, and later worked on staff at Ridgecrest Baptist Assembly in North Carolina. He also began preaching revivals and taking pastorates at local churches. He eventually enrolled in The Southwestern Baptist Theological Seminary, finishing his Bachelor of Divinity in 1957 and his Doctor of Theology in 1963. Here, he met his wife, Jean, and they were married on June 11, 1960.

Between his bachelor's and doctoral studies, Fish worked as a full-time evangelist, but upon beginning his second degree, he reentered the pastorate. While pastoring Live Oak Baptist Church in Gatesville, Texas, Fish received a clear call from the Lord that would not only affect the direction of his life, but also impact countless men and women who had been called to ministry.

"I was walking down a country road one Saturday night, thinking about my Sunday morning message," Fish later recalled. "It was dark, and I found myself aware of the Lord's presence. I started thinking about my reasons for working on a doctorate at Southwestern, and I suppose I asked out loud why I was beginning this advanced degree. It was almost as if the Lord Himself spoke audibly, saying, 'You are doing this because some day you will be teaching evangelism at Southwestern Seminary.'"

In 1965, then-president Robert Naylor offered Fish a position on Southwestern Seminary's faculty as a professor of evangelism. Considering this position one of the most strategic in the Kingdom of God, Fish gladly accepted and proceeded to serve at the institution for nearly 50 years, impacting the lives of thousands of students.

"In training young men and women to share the Gospel," Steve Fish said, "Dad found a calling in which God sustained him and our family with an inner blessing and vigor."

As an evangelism professor, Fish, who once occupied the seminary's Chair of Evangelism ("Chair of Fire"), instilled in the souls of thousands of God-called men and women a fire for evangelism. For many years, he also organized the annual Spring Break Revival Practicum (now called Revive This Nation), deploying hundreds of student preachers across the United States to preach revivals in local churches. He also wrote several evangelism resources for use in both the church and the classroom, including *Dare to Share* and *Giving a Good Invitation.*

"Few men have ever stood with more integrity and consistency over a lifetime," said Jimmy Draper, former president of LifeWay, who sat under Fish's preaching. "Whether as a pastor, a seminary professor, a conference speaker, or a friend, Roy Fish [was] God's instrument to motivate several generations to accept the challenge of the Great Commission."

"Perhaps no person in human history has taught evangelism to more ministerial students than Roy Fish," said Steve Gaines, pastor of Bellevue Baptist Church, who worked as a grader for Fish while a student at Southwestern Seminary. "... Through his preaching, writing, and teaching ministries, Fish has impacted a host of Christians and has encouraged and inspired them to sow the seed of the Gospel that they might reap the conversion of lost souls for Christ's glory."

Fish continued to preach revivals, fill interim pastorates, speak at conferences and convention meetings, and remain a personal soul-winner, but for the final 50 years of his life, he focused on encouraging others to be available witnesses for the Lord. When Southwestern Seminary later launched a school of evangelism and missions, it was named in honor of Roy J. Fish.

One oft-shared illustration reveals Fish's heart for evangelism. As an infant, Fish's son was chronically ill. One night, his cries awakened his father, so Fish took his infant son from his crib, gave him some medicine, and then rocked him back to sleep.

As he looked down at the precious face of his beloved son, Fish was struck with an alarming thought: "Suppose our little boy should die?

Suppose God should choose to make heaven richer by taking my son home to be with Him?"

As tears filled his eyes, Fish pondered why he felt this way. "It's not because I know this little fellow well, and he hardly knows me at all. Until a few months ago, he couldn't even recognize me in a crowd."

"Besides that," he continued, "we've never even had a conversation. I don't know how well we are going to get along.

"On top of that, there hasn't been a single night at home that he hasn't wakened me at least once and usually twice. Why should I care so much if this precious little bit of human flesh and spirit should go to be with God?"

Initially unable to articulate an answer to this question, Fish probed the matter, searching his soul for the reason. Finally, he discovered it: he realized that if his son should die at age 1, he would never know how much his father loved him.

The thought of this happening nearly broke Fish's heart.

Relating this story in *Dare to Share*, Fish said, "Love is like that, isn't it? Love desires to communicate. Love desires for response."

Applying this to the witnessing task, Fish concluded, "There is a Father in heaven who loves people so much that He sent His only Son to die on a cruel Roman cross for them. He loves every person. He wants every person to know about His love.

"God's love is like that. He desires people to know about it. But they will not know about it unless they hear about it from you and me. Our sharing is God's way for others to know about His love."

Fish used this illustration in his writing and preaching to provide insight into the character of God, who grieves because the lost who die without Christ never know how much He loves them. This experience taught Fish the importance of being an available witness for the Lord, and he shared the experience with others that they might do the same.

– Alex Sibley

WILLIAM B. TOLAR

When William B. Tolar's teacher challenged him to read the Bible, she had no idea the impact that challenge would have on not just the 13-year-old Tolar, but on generations of seminary students.

The teacher shared that the Bible was the best-selling book in history but speculated that 99 percent of people had never read it in its entirety. Tolar, not yet a Christian, accepted the challenge and started reading.

He quickly found himself convicted by the "living and effective" Word of God.

"I began to realize that if this book was right, then basically my life was wrong, because I was living without any serious regard for the God that the Scriptures were telling me about," Tolar later said.

This Bible reading set Tolar on a lifetime course of worship, Bible study, and teaching. He made his profession of faith on Easter Sunday in 1942, and a year later, he accepted the call to vocational ministry.

Tolar's academic and ministry career ultimately spanned more than half a century, and he came to be known as a world-renowned Bible teacher, a scholar among scholars, and a spiritual giant at The Southwestern Baptist Theological Seminary. But through it all, he sought only to serve the Lord by making an impact on individual lives.

"I had a very profound sense that I wanted my life to really count for God," he said of his initial calling. "If you were a minister, you would be helping people all the time."

William Bert Tolar was born on July 5, 1928, in Jonesboro, Louisiana. A successful student, he ranked highly in an academic competition and was named Louisiana's top high school running back. Louisiana State University offered him a full scholarship, but Tolar wanted to prepare for ministry at a Baptist school.

He graduated from Baylor University in 1950, and he was pastoring a nearby church when an educator again influenced his life. The chairman of Baylor's religion department asked if he would teach part-time. Tolar accepted, and a year later, he was offered a full-time position.

After teaching at Baylor for 10 years, Tolar came to Southwestern Seminary in 1965 with his wife, Floye, to teach and complete his Doctor of Theology degree. He was elected to the seminary faculty that same year as a distinguished professor of biblical backgrounds.

In the nearly four decades that followed, Tolar equipped thousands of Southwestern Seminary students for ministry around the world. These included many who would serve in pivotal roles in the Southern Baptist Convention, including Jimmy Draper, Ronnie Floyd, David S. Dockery, and the ninth president of Southwestern Seminary, Adam W. Greenway.

"Dr. Tolar set an example of how to combine academic theological education with practical ministry in the churches," said Russell Dilday, president of Southwestern Seminary from 1978-1994. "He was a preacher-minister, but he also was a scholarly professor, balancing the intellectual with practical service in the churches.

"And it was that balance of intellectual scholarship with practical application as a practicing minister—not just theoretical knowledge, but knowledge lived out in Christian service—that endeared him to students and to fellow academics, church ministers, and lay leaders alike. I think there are few people more widely known and respected in academic and local church life."

Tolar went on to serve as dean of the School of Theology and then as vice president for academic affairs and provost. In the late spring of 1994, Tolar was called to serve as the seminary's acting president until Ken Hemphill was hired later that year.

Writing in the May/June 1994 issue of Southwestern News, Tolar said of his role as acting president, "Quite frankly, I had great reluctance to serve in this capacity because my calling, training, and passion for nearly 40 years have been for teaching and preaching and not for administration. ... It was only because of my profound respect, love, and appreciation for the faculty, administration, staff, and the student body of the seminary that I agreed to accept these awesome responsibilities."

Tolar said his immediate goal as the acting president was "to redeem this spring semester for our entire seminary family—especially our graduating students."

In his column for the next magazine, Tolar reflected that this goal had been accomplished. "At the reception for the graduates held the night before spring commencement," he wrote, "almost every student who spoke to me expressed heartfelt gratitude for the way administrators, faculty, and staff had worked to make things go smoothly for them during the closing weeks of the semester."

Ken Hemphill, who was elected Southwestern Seminary's seventh president in late 1994, said Tolar's impact on the seminary was "immense."

"I think he was invaluable in that transition time; it was a pretty difficult time in the life of the institution," Hemphill said. "And I think he was a real peacemaker, scholar, and gentleman.

"When I came, he was very supportive of me being there, and that helped in the transition with existing faculty and students. And he not only helped me to understand some of the dynamics of the school, since I was not a Southwestern graduate myself, but also to know some of the history, some of the traditions of the school and the institution, to be able to connect with its past as well as to look to its future."

Following his tenure at Southwestern Seminary, Tolar taught as an adjunct professor at Dallas Baptist University and as a distinguished fellow at the B.H. Carroll Theological Institute. Throughout his ministry, Tolar studied and lectured in 53 countries and served as guest lecturer in the Holy Land more than 80 times. He also served as interim pastor at nearly 50 churches, including First Baptist Church in Dallas.

After his retirement, Tolar maintained an active teaching schedule at DBU. He and his wife also established the William B. and Floye Tolar Faculty Assistance Endowment Fund, which provides financial assistance to faculty and staff at Southwestern Seminary.

"Bill Tolar was my student, my faculty colleague, my dean, my vice president, my acting president, and my dear friend," said James Leo Garrett, distinguished professor emeritus of theology at Southwestern Seminary. "A clear witness to the grace of God, Dr. Tolar masterfully lectured on biblical backgrounds and preached and taught the Bible in scores of Southern Baptist churches. He was, in his generation, the preeminent conductor of tours to the biblical lands."

When news of Tolar's failing health began to spread in 2018, many of his former students took to social media to share memories of his influence. One student said, "Out of love for the Scriptures, often he would tear up as he taught the class."

Tolar died on December 29, 2018, leaving behind a legacy of biblical scholarship coupled with personal ministry, all in service to the Lord.

"Dr. Tolar's legacy of distinguished service at Southwestern Seminary is an example to every minister of the Gospel," said D. Jeffrey Bingham, dean of the School of Theology. "Whether in the classroom, as dean of the School of Theology, as vice president for academic affairs, as provost, or as acting president, Dr. Tolar faithfully served his Lord at his alma mater."

– Julie Owens and Alex Sibley

RESOURCES FOR
FURTHER STUDY

B.H. Carroll

B.H. Carroll Presidential Papers. Archives and Special Collections, J.T. and Zelma Luther Archives, Southwestern Baptist Theological Seminary, Fort Worth, Texas.

Baker, Robert A. *Tell The Generations Following: A History of Southwestern Baptist Theological Seminary 1908-1983.* Nashville, TN: Broadman Press, 1983, Chapters 2-4: 53-187.

Burroughs, P.E. "Benajah Harvey Carroll, Founder and First President, Southwestern Baptist Theological Seminary," in *Ten Men From Baylor*, ed. J.M. Price. Kansas City, KS: Central Seminary Press, 1945.

Carroll, B.H. *Baptists and Their Doctrines*, edited by Timothy and Denise George. Nashville, TN: Broadman & Holman Publishers, 1995.

Carroll, J.M. *Dr. B.H. Carroll, the Colossus of Baptist History: Pastor, First Baptist Church, Waco, Texas, and First President of S.W.B.T. Seminary, Fort Worth, Texas.* Fort Worth, TX: J.W. Crowder, 1946.

Crisp, Michael. "B.H. Carroll – Remembering His Life, Expanding His Legacy" in *Southwestern Journal of Theology* 58, no. 2 (Spring 2016): 159-181.

Lefever, Alan. *Fighting the Good Fight: The Life and Work of Benajah Harvey Carroll*. Austin, TX: Eakin Press, 1994.

Ray, Jeff. *B.H. Carroll*. Nashville, TN: Sunday School Board, 1927.

Segler, Franklin M. "B.H. Carroll: Model for Ministers" in *Southwestern Journal of Theology* 25, no. 2 (Spring 1983): 4-23.

_____. "Carroll, Benajah Harvey" in *Encyclopedia of Southern Baptists*. Nashville, TN: Broadman Press, 1958: 232-233.

Spivey, Jr. James T. "B.H. Carroll" in *The Legacy of Southwestern: Writings That Shaped a Tradition*. North Richland Hills, TX: Smithfield Press, 2002.

_____. "Benajah Harvey Carroll" in *Theologians of the Baptist Tradition*, edited by Timothy George and David S. Dockery. Nashville, TN: Broadman & Holman Publishers, 2001.

L.R. Scarborough

L.R. Scarborough Presidential Papers. Archives and Special Collections, J.T. and Zelma Luther Archives, Southwestern Baptist Theological Seminary, Fort Worth, Texas.

Baker, Robert A. *Tell The Generations Following: A History of Southwestern Baptist Theological Seminary 1908-1983*. Nashville, TN: Broadman Press, 1983, Chapters 5-6: 197-280.

Caner, Emir and Ergun. *The Sacred Trust: Sketches of the Southern Baptist Convention Presidents*. Nashville, TN: Broadman & Holman, 2003, Chapter 21: 83-86.

Carson, Glenn Thomas. *The Life and Work of Lee Rutland Scarborough*. Austin, TX: Eakin Press, 1996.

Crowell, Evelyn Miller. "Dr. Lee Rutland Scarborough: A Memorial" in *Men of Achievement: Texas Edition*. Dallas, TX: John Moranz Associates, 1948: 162-163.

Dana, H.E. *Lee Rutland Scarborough: A Life of Service*. Nashville, TN: Broadman Press, 1942.

_____. "Lee Rutland Scarborough, President of Southwestern Baptist Theological Seminary, and Southern Baptist Convention" in *Ten Men From Baylor*, ed. J.M. Price. Kansas City, KS: Central Seminary Press, 1945.

Foreman, Jr. A.D. "The Evangelistic Thrust of L.R. Scarborough" in *Southwestern Journal of Theology* 7, no. 1 (October 1964): 54-62.

Fish, Roy J. "Lee Rutland Scarborough" in *The Legacy of Southwestern: Writings That Shaped a Tradition*. North Richland Hills, TX: Smithfield Press, 2002.

Nettles, Thomas J. "L.R. Scarborough: Public Figure" in *Southwestern Journal of Theology* 25, no. 2 (Spring 1983): 24-42.

Segler, Franklin. "Scarborough, Lee Rutland" in *Encyclopedia of Southern Baptists*. Nashville, TN: Broadman Press, 1958: 1186-1187.

J.B. Gambrell

J.B. Gambrell Faculty File. Archives and Special Collections, J.T. and Zelma Luther Archives, Southwestern Baptist Theological Seminary, Fort Worth, Texas.

Caner, Emir and Ergun. *The Sacred Trust: Sketches of the Southern Baptist Convention Presidents*. Nashville, TN: Broadman & Holman, 2003, Chapter 13: 48-52.

McBeth, Harry Leon. *Texas Baptists: A Sesquicentennial History*. Dallas, TX: Baptistway Press, 1998: 95-96.

Routh, E.C. "Gambrell, James Bruton" in *Encyclopedia of Southern Baptists*. Nashville, TN: Broadman Press, 1958: 522-523.

_____. *The Life Story of Dr. J.B. Gambrell*. Oklahoma City, OK: The Author, 1929.

Winters, A.G. "James B. Gambrell (1841-1921)" in *A Noble Company: Biographical Essays on Notable Particular-Regular Baptists in America, Volume Eleven*, ed. Terry Wolever. Springfield, MO: Particular Baptist Press, 2018: 332-355.

George W. Truett

George W. Truett Papers. Archives and Special Collections, J.T. and Zelma Luther Archives, Southwestern Baptist Theological Seminary, Fort Worth, Texas.

Burton, Joe W. *Prince of the Pulpit: A Pen Picture of George W. Truett at Work*. Grand Rapids, MI: Zondervan, 1946.

Caner, Emir and Ergun. *The Sacred Trust: Sketches of the Southern Baptist Convention Presidents*. Nashville, TN: Broadman & Holman, 2003, Chapter 16: 61-65.

Crowell, Evelyn Miller. "Dr. George W. Truett: A Memorial" in *Men of Achievement: Texas Edition*. Dallas, TX: John Moranz Associates, 1948: 160-161.

Durso, Keith E. *Thy Will Be Done: A Biography of George W. Truett*. Macon, GA: Mercer University Press, 2009.

James, Powhatan. *George W. Truett: A Biography*. New York: Macmillan Company, 1939.

_____. "George W. Truett, Pastor, President Southern Baptist Convention, and Baptist World Alliance" in *Ten Men From Baylor*, ed. J.M. Price. Kansas City, KS: Central Seminary Press, 1945.

_____. "Truett, George Washington" in *Encyclopedia of Southern Baptists*. Nashville, TN: Broadman Press, 1958: 1429-1430.

McBeth, Leon. *The First Baptist Church of Dallas: Centennial History, 1868-1968*. Grand Rapids: Zondervan, 1968.

Young, Doyle L. "Leadership That Motivates: A Study in the Life of George W. Truett" in *Baptist History and Heritage* 20, no. 1 (January 1985): 45-51.

J. Frank Norris

J. Frank Norris Papers. Archives and Special Collections, J.T. and Zelma Luther Archives, Southwestern Baptist Theological Seminary, Fort Worth, Texas.

Entzminger, Louis. *The J. Frank Norris I Have Known For 34 Years.* Np. Np. 1948.

Hankins, Barry. *God's Rascal: J. Frank Norris and the Beginnings of Southern Fundamentalism.* Lexington, KY: The University Press of Kentucky, 1996.

McBeth, Leon. "J. Frank Norris and Southwestern Seminary" in *Southwestern Journal of Theology* 30, no. 3 (Summer 1988): 14-19.

Morris, Gwin. "Frank Norris: Rascal or Reformer?" in *Baptist History and Heritage* 33, no. 3 (Autumn 1998): 21-40.

Norris, J. Frank. *The Inside History of First Baptist Church, Fort Worth and Temple Baptist Church, Detroit: The Life Story of Dr. J. Frank Norris.* Np. Np. 1938.

Stokes, David R. *Apparent Danger: The Pastor of America's First Megachurch and the Texas Murder Trial of the Decade in the 1920s.* Minneapolis: Bascom Hill Books, 2010.

_____. *The Shooting Salvationist: J. Frank Norris and the Murder Trial That Captivated America.* Hanover, NH: Steerforth Press, 2011.

Taylor, Wilburn S. "Norris, John Franklyn" in *Encyclopedia of Southern Baptists.* Nashville, TN: Broadman Press, 1958: 983.

W.T. Conner

W.T. Conner Papers. Archives and Special Collections, J.T. and Zelma Luther Archives, Southwestern Baptist Theological Seminary, Fort Worth, Texas.

Garrett, Jr. James Leo. "The Bible at Southwestern Seminary During Its Formative Years: A Study of H.E. Dana and W.T. Conner" in *Baptist History and Heritage* 21, no. 4 (October 1986): 29-43.

_____. "Walter Thomas Conner" in *The Legacy of Southwestern: Writings That Shaped a Tradition*. North Richland Hills, TX: Smithfield Press, 2002.

_____. "Walter Thomas Conner" in *Theologians of the Baptist Tradition*, edited by Timothy George and David S. Dockery. Nashville, TN: Broadman & Holman Publishers, 2001.

_____. "W.T. Conner: Contemporary Theologian" in *Southwestern Journal of Theology* 25, no. 2 (Spring 1983): 43-60.

Newman, Stewart A. *W.T. Conner: Theologian of the Southwest.* Nashville, TN: Broadman Press, 1964.

Northcutt, Jesse J. "Walter Thomas Conner, Theologian of Southwestern" in *Southwestern Journal of Theology* 9, no. 1 (Fall 1966): 81-89.

I.E. Reynolds

I.E. Reynolds Papers. Archives and Special Collections, J.T. and Zelma Luther Archives, Southwestern Baptist Theological Seminary, Fort Worth, Texas.

Carnett, Ellis L. "Isham Emmanuel Reynolds: God's Servant in Church Music" in *Southwestern Journal of Theology* 10, no. 2 (Spring 1969): 85-93.

Reynolds, I.E. "Autobiographical Sketch" in *Southwestern Men and Their Messages*, ed. J.M. Price. Kansas City, KS: Central Seminary Press, 1948: 109-111.

Reynolds, William J. *The Cross & The Lyre: The Story of the School of Church Music, Southwestern Baptist Theological Seminary, Fort Worth, Texas*. Fort Worth, TX: Faculty of the School of Church Music, SWBTS, 1994.

_____. "I.E. Reynolds: Southern Baptist Church Music Crusader" in *Southwestern Journal of Theology* 25, no. 2 (Spring 1983): 76-88.

_____. "Isham Emmanuel Reynolds: Church Musician" in *Baptist History and Heritage* 27, no. 2 (April 1992): 31-41.

Thompson, Sarah. "Reynolds, Isham Emmanuel" in *Encyclopedia of Southern Baptists*. Nashville, TN: Broadman Press, 1958: 1164.

J.M. Price

J.M. Price Papers. Archives and Special Collections, J.T. and Zelma Luther Archives, Southwestern Baptist Theological Seminary, Fort Worth, Texas.

Heacock, Joe Davis. "J.M. Price: Trailblazer in Religious Education" in *Southwestern Journal of Theology* 17, no. 1 (Fall 1974): 83-94.

Maguire, Clyde Merrill. *J.M. Price: Portrait of a Pioneer*. Nashville, TN: Broadman Press, 1960.

Marsh, Leon. "J.M. Price: Pioneer in Religious Education" in *Southwestern Journal of Theology* 25, no. 2 (Spring 1983): 61-75.

Smith, William A. "John Milburn Price" in *The Legacy of Southwestern: Writings That Shaped a Tradition.* North Richland Hills, TX: Smithfield Press, 2002.

Terry, Jr. Jack D. *Christian Education on the Plains of Texas: A History of the School of Religious Education at Southwestern Baptist Theological Seminary, 1915-2015.* Fort Worth, TX: Seminary Hill Press, 2018.

T.B. Maston

T.B. Maston Papers. Archives and Special Collections, J.T. and Zelma Luther Archives, Southwestern Baptist Theological Seminary, Fort Worth, Texas.

Goff, William E. "Thomas Buford Maston" in *The Legacy of Southwestern: Writings That Shaped a Tradition.* North Richland Hills, TX: Smithfield Press, 2002.

Martin, Earl R. *Passport to Servanthood: The Life and Missionary Influence of T.B. Maston.* Nashville, TN: Broadman Press, 1988.

Maston, T.B. *Oral Memoirs of T.B. Maston.* Interviewer Rufus B. Spain. Baylor University Program for Oral History. Waco, TX: Baylor University Religion and Culture Project, 1973.

Pinson, Jr. William M., ed. *An Approach to Christian Ethics: The Life, Contribution, and Thought of T.B. Maston.* Nashville, TN: Broadman Press, 1979.

_____. "Texas Baptist Contributions to Ethics: The Life and Influence of T.B. Maston" in *Baptist History and Heritage* 33, no. 3 (Autumn 1998): 7-20.

Valentine, Foy. "T.B. Maston: A Conscience for Southern Baptists" in *Southwestern Journal of Theology* 25, no. 2 (Spring 1983): 89-103.

Floy Barnard

Floy Barnard Faculty File. Archives and Special Collections, J.T. and Zelma Luther Archives, Southwestern Baptist Theological Seminary, Fort Worth, Texas.

Baker, Robert A. *Tell The Generations Following: A History of Southwestern Baptist Theological Seminary 1908-1983*. Nashville, TN: Broadman Press, 1983.

Barnard, Floy. [Untitled autobiographical manuscript delivered to the Texas Women's Missionary Union]. Floy Barnard Faculty File. Archives and Special Collections, J.T. and Zelma Luther Archives, Southwestern Baptist Theological Seminary, Fort Worth, Texas.

Billings, Diane F. "A Virtuous Woman: The Life of Dr. Floy M. Barnard" (Unpublished paper). Floy Barnard Faculty File. Archives and Special Collections, J.T. and Zelma Luther Archives, Southwestern Baptist Theological Seminary, Fort Worth, Texas.

Keith, Billy. "Floy Barnard Retires After 27 Years," *Southwestern News*, May 1960, 3.

Koob, Rose Mary. "Dr. Floy Barnard recalls experiences as educator, author," Greeley (Colo.) Tribune, August 3, 1976, 12.

Price, J.M. [Biographical Sketch of Floy M. Barnard]. Floy Barnard Faculty File. Archives and Special Collections, J.T. and Zelma Luther Archives, Southwestern Baptist Theological Seminary, Fort Worth, Texas.

Terry, Jr. Jack D. *Christian Education on the Plains of Texas: A History of the School of Religious Education at Southwestern Baptist Theological Seminary, 1915-2015*. Fort Worth, TX: Seminary Hill Press, 2018.

E.D. Head

E.D. Head Presidential Papers. Archives and Special Collections, J.T. and Zelma Luther Archives, Southwestern Baptist Theological Seminary, Fort Worth, Texas.

Baker, Robert A. *Tell The Generations Following: A History of Southwestern Baptist Theological Seminary 1908-1983*. Nashville, TN: Broadman Press, 1983, Chapter 7: "A Shining New Day," 285-323.

Crowell, Evelyn Miller. "Eldred Douglas Head, President of Southwestern Baptist Theological Seminary" in *Men of Achievement: Texas Edition*. Dallas, TX: John Moranz Associates, 1948: 164-165.

McBeth, Harry Leon. *Texas Baptists: A Sesquicentennial History*. Dallas, TX: Baptistway Press, 1998.

J. Howard Williams

J. Howard Williams Presidential Papers. Archives and Special
Collections, J.T. and Zelma Luther Archives, Southwestern
Baptist Theological Seminary, Fort Worth, Texas.

Baker, Robert A. *Tell The Generations Following: A History of
Southwestern Baptist Theological Seminary 1908-1983*. Nashville,
TN: Broadman Press, 1983, Chapter 8: "Five Golden Years,"
329-361.

Brown, Jr. H.C. and Charles P. Johnson, compilers and editors. *J.
Howard Williams: Prophet of God and Friend of Man*. San Antonio,
TX: Naylor Co., 1963.

McBeth, Harry Leon. *Texas Baptists: A Sesquicentennial History*.
Dallas, TX: Baptistway Press, 1998: 192-193, 196-198.

Robert E. Naylor

Robert E. Naylor Presidential Papers. Archives and Special
Collections, J.T. and Zelma Luther Archives, Southwestern
Baptist Theological Seminary, Fort Worth, Texas.

Baker, Robert A. *Tell The Generations Following: A History of
Southwestern Baptist Theological Seminary 1908-1983*. Nashville,
TN: Broadman Press, 1983, Chapter 9: "Unprecedented Growth,"
371-436.

_____. "The Retirement of President Robert E. Naylor" in
Southwestern Journal of Theology 20, no. 2 (Spring 1978): 7-14.

McBeth, Harry Leon. *Texas Baptists: A Sesquicentennial History.* Dallas, TX: Baptistway Press, 1998.

Naylor, Robert E. *A Messenger's Memoirs: Sixty-One Southern Baptist Convention Meetings.* Franklin, TN: Providence House Publishers, 1995.

John Earl Seelig

John Earl Seelig Faculty File. Archives and Special Collections, J.T. and Zelma Luther Archives, Southwestern Baptist Theological Seminary, Fort Worth, Texas.

Edwards, Frances. "Director of News Named For Baptist Japan Crusade," Fort Worth Star-Telegram, December 8, 1962.

Sibley, Alex. "Former VP of public affairs John Seelig dies," Southwestern Baptist Theological Seminary Press Release, January 18, 2019.

Roy J. Fish

Roy J. Fish Papers. Archives and Special Collections, J.T. and Zelma Luther Archives, Southwestern Baptist Theological Seminary, Fort Worth, Texas.

Collier, Keith. "Roy Fish 'loved all the right things,'" Southern Baptist Texan, October 1, 2012.

Fish, Steve. "A Profile of Roy Fish" in *Evangelism for a Changing World*, ed. Timothy Beougher and Alvin Reid. Wheaton, IL: Harold Shaw Publishers, 1995: 263-274.

Gaines, Steve. "Eulogy for Dr. Roy Fish, Friday, September 14, 2012" (Unpublished). Roy J. Fish Faculty File. Archives and Special Collections, J.T. and Zelma Luther Archives, Southwestern Baptist Theological Seminary, Fort Worth, Texas.

_____. "Professional History" in *Evangelism for a Changing World*, ed. Timothy Beougher and Alvin Reid. Wheaton, IL: Harold Shaw Publishers, 1995: 275-282.

Jones, Jim. "Fish influenced growing world of evangelists," Fort Worth Star-Telegram, September 14, 2012, 8B.

Stetzer, Ed. "Remembering Roy Fish on the Anniversary of His Passing." The Exchange (blog). September 2013. Roy J. Fish Faculty File. Archives and Special Collections, J.T. and Zelma Luther Archives, Southwestern Baptist Theological Seminary, Fort Worth, Texas.

William B. Tolar

William B. Tolar Faculty File. Archives and Special Collections, J.T. and Zelma Luther Archives, Southwestern Baptist Theological Seminary, Fort Worth, Texas.

Druin, Toby. "'Tolar named acting president at seminary," The Baptist Standard, April 6, 1994: 3, 10.

Johnson, Kaley. "Bible scholar remembered for a lifetime of service to others," Fort Worth Star-Telegram, January 13, 2019, 1B-2B.

Roach, David. "Bill Tolar, prof who 'stands large' in SBC, dies," Baptist Press, January 2, 2019.

Smith, Samuel. "Bill Tolar [Faculty Retirement]," *Southwestern News*, Summer 2003, 45.